More advance praise for
Now, Build a Great Business!

"No one can give you clearer advice about how to run a great company than Mark Thompson and Brian Tracy. *Now, Build a Great Business!* is the perfect prescription for a much more profitable and personally rewarding business."

—Keith Ferrazzi, #1 *New York Times* bestselling author
of *Who's Got Your Back* and *Never Eat Alone*

"Now, Build a Great Business! is the perfect balance between how-to and practical wisdom. Mark Thompson and Brian Tracy have crafted an inspirational book that will allow leaders and organizations to achieve their goals."

—Tab Nkhereanye, Sony/ATV Music

"Mark and Brian give you an insider's look at what happens when you show more genuine caring for your customers and employees. Everybody wins! You'll enjoy this book, but most importantly, use this book!"

—John Christensen, bestselling coauthor of *FISH!*

"The ideas, strategies, and tactics in this book will catapult you from where you are to where you want to be, faster and easier than ever before."

—John Assaraf, *New York Times* bestselling author of *The Answer*

"'Breakthrough' is an overused word, though I can think of none more appropriate to describe Brian Tracy and Mark Thompson's new book, *Now, Build a Great Business!* It should be mandatory reading for everyone in business . . . including billionaires."

—Bill Bartmann, self-made billionaire and CEO, Bill Bartmann Enterprises

"Mark Thompson and Brian Tracy are two great business coaches I've long admired who've joined forces to bring you a book with the leadership tools you need to *Build a Great Business.*"

—Dr. Steven Stargardter, President, John F. Kennedy University

"Mark Thompson and Brian Tracy's tremendous research, based on Mark's first-hand discussions with many of the most successful business luminaries of our time, give an informed perspective unique in the marketplace. Mark is the *Napoleon Hill* of the 21st Century and Brian is the *Dale Carnegie.*"

—Greg Link, cofounder, CoveyLink; producer of the *New York Times* bestseller, *The Speed of Trust,* with Stephen M.R. Covey

"*Now, Build a Great Business!* is a compelling read and gives you decades of hard-earned business experience presented in a way that is easy to implement. I love this book because it is so practical. The more people who read it, the faster we will get back to prosperity for self and shareholders!"

—Julie Woods-Moss, business strategist and former President, British Telecom Strategy and Marketing

"I help people and organizations achieve their full potential. In *Now, Build a Great Business!*, Mark Thompson and Brian Tracy demonstrate that growing extraordinary people is the only way to deliver extraordinary results."

—Stephen Miles, Vice Chairman, Heidrick & Struggles

"An incredible book for jumpstarting growth, supercharging teams, and taking your business to a whole new level of growth. This year's best read on growth and profitability!"

—Jason Jennings, *New York Times* bestselling author of *Less Is More, Think BIG-Act Small,* and *Hit the Ground Running*

"Imagine having lunch with the greatest leaders of our time and asking them what mattered (and what didn't), so that you could apply it to your life's work. This is what Mark Thompson and Brian Tracy have been doing for decades. This book gives you a seat at the table—an amazing gift that empowers you to succeed in ways that endure."

—David Jeffers, Retail Brand Experience, John Deere

"Mark and Brian teach you to build a successful business and life with clarity and care. Reading their words is like plugging into your personal battery charger. You will find the encouragement to become the unique leader you are meant to be."

—Alex von Bidder, Managing Partner and co-owner, The Four Seasons Restaurant

"I have long since marveled and respected Brian Tracy and Mark Thompson for all of their business and life wisdom. You will find this book relevant, powerful, clear, and practical. This will surely help many leaders fine-tune their businesses and help create some brand new ones bound for greatness!"

—Steve Rodgers, President/Owner, Windermere Properties; former CEO, Prudential California Realty, a division of Berkshire Hathaway

"Mark and Brian are thoughtful, experienced leaders who've created a great read without the usual hype from management books. It's just the right perspective to grow your business."

—Mike Linton, Forbes.com columnist; former CMO, Best Buy and eBay

"Leaders wishing to take their businesses to the next level should soak up the down-to-earth prescription in Mark Thompson and Brian Tracy's *Now, Build a Great Business!* This book captures what it really takes. Do it now!"

—Minter Dial, Brand Strategist and former member of the L'Oréal Executive Committee and Worldwide General Manager of Redken 5th Avenue NYC

"Mark Thompson and Brian Tracy are among the world's thought leaders, and this amazing book proves it with its transformational ability to make your business profitable and built to last!"

—Chet Holmes, bestselling author of *The Ultimate Sales Machine*; CEO, BusinessBreakthroughs.com

"We are in the Era of the Entrepreneur. NOW is your time to profit, and *Now, Build a Great Business!* is the instruction manual you have been waiting for on how to do it. Every page is chock-full with practical and actionable strategies you will continually refer to in your ascent to entrepreneurial greatness."

—Darren Hardy, Publisher, *SUCCESS magazine*

"Leadership in building a business is about character, competence, and perseverance. These are traits that describe Mark Thompson and Brian Tracy, and that's what you will learn from them when you read this great book."

—Karen Chang, business adviser and former President, Charles Schwab Individual Investor Enterprise

Now, Build 'a Great Business!

Now, Build 'a Great Business!

7 Ways to Maximize Your Profits in Any Market

Mark Thompson
and Brian Tracy

Foreword by Frances Hesselbein,
President and CEO, Leader to Leader Institute

AMACOM

American Management Association
New York • Atlanta • Brussels • Chicago • Mexico City • San Francisco
Shanghai • Tokyo • Toronto • Washington, D.C.

Bulk discounts available. For details visit:
www.amacombooks.org/go/specialsales
Or contact special sales:
Phone: 800-250-5308
Email: specialsls@amanet.org
View all the AMACOM titles at: www.amacombooks.org

Library of Congress Cataloging-in-Publication Data

Thompson, Mark.
  Now, build a great business! : 7 ways to maximize your profits in any market / Mark Thompson and Brian Tracy ; foreword by Frances Hesselbein.—1st ed.
    p.   cm.
  Includes index.
  ISBN-13: 978-0-8144-1697-6
  ISBN-10: 0-8144-1697-7
  1. Leadership.   2. Strategic planning.   3. Marketing.   4. Consumer satisfaction.   I. Tracy, Brian.   II. Title.
HD57.7.T46734   2011
658—dc22

                                                              2010030612

About AMA

American Management Association (www.amanet.org) is a world leader in talent development, advancing the skills of individuals to drive business success. Our mission is to support the goals of individuals and organizations through a complete range of products and services, including classroom and virtual seminars, webcasts, webinars, podcasts, conferences, corporate and government solutions, business books, and research. AMA's approach to improving performance combines experiential learning—learning through doing—with opportunities for ongoing professional growth at every step of one's career journey.

Printing number

10   9   8   7   6   5   4   3   2   1

To Barbara and Bonita, and our families,
whose lives have transformed
and enriched our own beyond measure

Contents

CONTENTS

Foreword

Peter Drucker famously taught that "the purpose of a business is to create and keep a customer." He emphasized the importance of customer satisfaction as the true measure of success in every organization.

The central theme of this book is what you must do as an entrepreneur or executive to trigger the customer response, *This is a great product!* As Drucker inspired us to ask, "What does the customer value?"

Fully 90 percent of your organization's success in these turbulent times will be determined by how often and how consistently you can serve your customers with excellence.

Now, Build a Great Business! shows you how to build your organization by focusing on great leadership, great people, and great products.

Success is the result of doing the right things over and over again, and this book shows you how you can measure your progress in every area, at every stage of your strategy.

My friends Mark Thompson and Brian Tracy know what it takes for the best leaders to achieve success with courage, integrity, and consistency. I have had the pleasure of working with them over the years and have come to deeply respect their knowledge and business acumen, and most important, their heartfelt commitment to serving others.

"To serve is to live," is not a foreign concept to Mark and Brian. They are two great thought leaders.

This indispensible handbook for success gives you a practical track to run on, enabling you to inspire your organization to grow faster because you are serving customers better, with greater predictability, than ever before. Enjoy this great book as you "build a great business!"

Frances Hesselbein
Cofounder, President, and CEO, Leader to Leader
Institute, and Chair, Study of Leadership at the
U.S. Military Academy, West Point

Preface

Are you ready to reignite growth in your business? Are you willing to take bold new action to attract better people and win more profitable customers?

If so, where can you go for unbiased advice? The challenge for most leaders today is finding practical, down-to-earth coaching on the strategies and actions necessary to grow your company quickly and efficiently—without the opaque philosophy and clever but useless sound bites that most consultants will give you.

In this book, you will find brilliantly easy, battle-tested ways to think about every step of the process of supercharging growth in your organization in just the right sequence. Without hype or academic complexity, you'll see exactly what needs to be done and how to do it, and gain a whole new perspective on your future.

In seven fundamental steps, business growth experts Mark Thompson and Brian Tracy will help you and your team develop sustainable strategies for attracting great customers and recruiting better leaders to serve them. You will explore the subtleties of creating more useful plans that have worked for other great managers and entrepreneurs.

You'll see just how easily you can create or destroy a lasting customer experience and discover how to set better priorities in your business in just the areas that matter most to your customers.

Most important, *Now, Build a Great Business!* offers seven deceptively simple questions to ask yourself and your team. If taken to heart, these questions can save you substantial time, money, and heartache. They could make or break your business.

Most leaders don't realize soon enough that the most critical time to explore these issues—and to *grow your company and career*—is when the world appears to be spinning apart. It is when competitors are struggling to keep pace with rapid changes that the greatest opportunities emerge and, in many cases, the most profitable and longest lasting organizations get their groove back or find their *mojo*. Right now is the best time ever for you to set yourself apart.

This book is designed to help you address the questions that matter most to the future of your business—and to your own ultimate success.

What are you waiting for? Now, *Go* Build a Great Business!

Marshall Goldsmith
New York Times bestselling author of *Mojo* and *What Got You Here Won't Get You There,* and one of the Forbes "top 50 business thinkers in the world"

Acknowledgments

Twenty years ago, Peter Drucker and Frances Hesselbein founded what is today called the Leader to Leader Institute. It was a culmination of their lifetime of research on management and their service to emerging leaders in the social sector and all over the world. It is a great honor to be of service to the board of governors of the Institute and to support its mission in every aspect of our personal and professional lives. That's what made this book possible.

We have had the privilege of learning from and working with thousands of successful leaders whose contributions have inspired millions of people to do more and be more than they could ever imagine. We want to thank everyone whose ideas and insights made this journey possible.

We are grateful for this collaboration with the American Management Association, and we greatly admire their bold leadership in this field. We give special thanks to our Amacom editors, Ellen Kadin and Barry Richardson, and their team, especially Chris Murray and James Bessent, for their guidance and extraordinary commitment to excellence.

Jim Collins and Frances Hesselbein urged Mark Thompson, during the inauguration of the Hesselbein Global Academy, to move faster on this book. They encouraged us to get these ideas out to emerging leaders who are ready and willing to drive forward with courage in turbulent times.

We appreciate the remarkable lessons and patient mentoring of world-class thought leaders Charles "Chuck" Schwab, Tony Robbins, Keith Ferrazzi, Peter Guber, Marshall Goldsmith, Jack Welch, Michael Dell, Mutual of America's Fred Altstadt, Julie Woods-Moss, Susanne Lyons, Karen Chang, George Lichter, Chet Holmes, John Assaraf, Jason Jennings, Jack Canfield, Harvey Mackay, T. Harv Eker, Mark Victor Hansen, Bill Bartmann, Randy Williams at Keiretsu Forum, Mike Maples, Nokia's Henry Tirri, Steve Rodgers, Bob Ackerman, Jeff Webber, Mike Linton, Larry Benet, Joel Barker, Doug Schallau, Sen. John McCain, Steve Miles at Heidrick & Struggles, Alex von Bidder at the Four Seasons, Lon O'Neil at the Society for Human Resource Management (SHRM), Tony Bingham at the American Society for Training & Development (ASTD), Howard Moskowitz, Joe Scarlett, Minter Dial, Gen. Gale Pollock (ret), Kevin Small, Chris Fralic, Geneva Johnson, Darlyne Bailey, Smule's Ge Wang and Jeff Smith, and Teri Whitcraft at ABC News—our cherished friends who shine a brighter light on how we can all be more effective and happier as leaders.

Thank you Alan Mulally, Ford Motor's gifted leader, for your generous time with us and your joyful and disciplined focus on showing what really matters in every organization.

Our pals at Stanford University, particularly professors Byron Reeves and Cliff Nass, supported this effort with research resources to better understand what it means to engage people in their work with greater meaning.

Thank you to Bonita Buell-Thompson, who was also the research director for the international bestseller, *Success Built to Last,* and whose expert counsel and analysis we cherish.

Sir Richard Branson joined the launch of this project with a generous spirit. He was among those who encouraged us to take action on this book in the first place. More important, he has inspired managers both in business and the social sector with Virgin Unite's public service work to enrich lives in every corner of the world.

We are grateful to Chelsea Frederick, Julie Dominy, and the entire team at Brian Tracy International—you all stepped up to support this book with all your passion and expertise.

Our thanks to entrepreneurial leaders IKEA's Ingvar Kamprad, Jeff Bezos at Amazon, Tony Hsieh at Zappos, and Ed Reilly at the American Management Association. When you listen to leaders like these, you can't help but be inspired to grow and contribute. They will be the first to tell you, "Now, go build a great business!"

Mark Thompson and Brian Tracy

Introduction

The time for theory is over. The time for action is now. We are in the midst of business turbulence and turmoil greater than we have ever seen before. Economic storms end, as they always do, but we will never go back to the good old ways of doing business. Today, competition is fiercer and more determined than ever. The challenges are greater and more demanding. The only way to survive and thrive will be to build a great business that can withstand the economic shocks of any market and rise to the top of its industry.

The market is flooded with business books that describe what an excellent business should look like. Descriptive information is enlightening and inspirational. It makes you want to be like the ideal leader running the ideal businesses they describe.

This book is different. It is deliberately prescriptive. It explains the seven keys to business greatness and exactly what you have to do to achieve them. No theory, just practical steps you can take immediately, with clear explanations of exactly how you can measure how well you are doing at each step along the way.

You'll learn what to do, how to do it, and the key numbers

you need to watch each day and month. You'll learn how to set clear targets and attach them to meaningful metrics. You will learn the very best, practical, and proven strategies and techniques practiced by the top businesses in every industry, with the goal of building a high-energy, high-morale, high-profit business of your own.

This book will show you how to attract customers, keep them coming back, and have them bring their friends. It tells you how to focus and concentrate your time, money, and resources on the most profitable products, services, and activities.

This book reveals how you can achieve better, more predictable results, especially financial results, faster than before. And how you can create a culture of continuous improvement to develop a lead over your competitors, and then continually widen that lead. As you learn how to move from wherever you are to wherever you want to be in the future, along the way you'll also see how to measure each critical variable and how to improve in each essential area. Especially, you'll learn how to trigger the same response, over and over, by people inside and outside your company, who will say . . .

"This is a great business!"

This book gives you a series of clear, simple, practical, and powerful methods and techniques you can use to build a great business in any market and in the face of any competition. Let's begin.

Mark Thompson and Brian Tracy

Now, Build 'a Great Business!

Become a Great Leader

"Faith is not simply a patience that passively suffers until the storm is past. Rather, it is a spirit that bears things—with resignations, yes, but above all with blazing serene hope."

—CORAZON AQUINO

Leadership is the most important requirement for business success. In simplest terms, leadership is the willingness to be accountable for results, and then to fulfill that responsibility, no matter what the external situation or pressure.

A leader is someone who is willing to do what it takes to get great things done. It doesn't happen on the first or second try. Leaders expect to fail over and over. They don't like it, but they don't quit when things don't work out. In fact, it is during difficult economic times and major crises that your character as a leader really stands out.

Why? In tough times, your competitors run for safety and survival instead of focusing on their customers. They pay less attention to quality. They slash back service and invest less in innovation. They cut back on staff at all levels. As a result, there are more great people actually available to work with you.

It is usually in a crisis that organizations reconnect with what made them great in the first place. In a crisis, leaders must make bolder decisions that will make them great in the future. It was said that "the North wind made the Vikings." In times of crisis, you have an opportunity to reignite your spirit and find better ways to delight your customers.

Your Leadership Matters

Today, more than ever, your leadership is needed. It is now time for you to step up in a new way. It is time for you to counterattack, to move forward, to innovate, to find better, faster, easier, cheaper ways to get results.

What you choose to do today—right now, in this market—can have more of an impact on your company and career than at any other time. Epictetus wrote: "Circumstances do not make the man; they only reveal him to himself."

Your ability to take charge, make hard decisions, accept responsibility, and lead effectively can have a greater impact on the success of your team or your organization than any other single factor. Everything that you do to become a more effective leader has a multiplication effect on your entire organization.

The Best and the Worst of Times

People often complain about the economy or the competition being tough, but many of the *best* leaders started their organizations at the *worst* possible time or steered them through the most difficult circumstances.

The 1970s plunged America into an era of "stagflation," with a combination of high interest rates, inflated gas prices, and miserable stock and real estate markets. It was considered a *lost decade*, much like the recent one we just endured.

Yet the 1970s were a time when great entrepreneurs did the unthinkable. Amid terrorist threats, massive bankruptcies, long gas lines, deregulation, and market bubbles, entrepreneurs like Charles Schwab, Steve Jobs, and Herb Kelleher each came to an extraordinary conclusion.

They decided: This is a great time to build a company!

Timing Is Overrated

Whether you are a Nobel Laureate like Muhammad Yunus or Nelson Mandela or an entrepreneur like Richard Branson or Oprah Winfrey, you don't wait for the "right time" to start something. Alan Mulally didn't just accept a job at Ford; he leaped at a huge opportunity to take the helm and make a difference when the company and *his country* needed him most.

Visionaries have a surprising knack for diving in at what appear to be the least propitious times. When you actually look at the environment in which they embraced their organizations, they often chose what competitors considered to be the worst possible time. Many people, looking from the outside, think these visionaries had it easy and perfectly set. Nothing could be further from the truth.

Opportunity in a Crisis

Walt Disney, Bill Hewlett and David Packard, Tom Watson (of IBM), and Thomas Edison (when he created his vision for Gen-

3

eral Electric)—all launched their dreams in miserable markets. FedEx, Sports Illustrated, Hyatt, Wikipedia, MTV, and Trader Joe's opened their doors just in time for awful recessions that defeated many other organizations. Even Google incorporated just in time for the tech bubble to burst at the end of the last century.

Leon Charney bought his first building the night Jimmy Carter lost his reelection bid to Ronald Reagan in 1980. Interest rates were in the double digits, and real estate was a bust. He plowed his rental income into twelve surrounding buildings, investing in 1.4 million square feet at Times Square. It never occurred to him that he'd become a billionaire and, today, one of the newer members of the Forbes 400 list, despite the current epic real estate slump.

Wang Chuanfu started BYD (Build Your Dream) after the dot-com crash to make advanced battery products when no one cared about the ex-professor's fantasy of a green, emission-free, battery-powered electric car. Warren Buffett bought 10 percent of BYD in 2008, making Chuanfu a billionaire and China's richest person.

False Starts

Many long-lasting organizations not only were born in bad markets, they also had unpopular products in the beginning. The list of short-lived, false starts for great companies is very, very long. It seems that business success is built on earlier failures.

There are plenty of legendary examples. Apple's Newton PDA was too bulky and expensive to succeed way back in 1993, but it paved the way for Research in Motion to bring the Blackberry to market and for Nokia to make smart phones a huge success long before Apple's iPhone.

Hewlett-Packard is at the top of its game today, growing at a feverish pace and overtaking rival Dell to become No. 1 in market share in PCs. But it didn't start out that way. Among its first electronic products was a device to make urinals flush automatically and a "shock" machine for dieters. Both were busts.

Humble Beginnings

One of Fortune's most admired companies in 2010, Marriott, didn't start as a hotel; it was an A&W root beer stand. Procter & Gamble began as just one of eighteen candle makers in Cincinnati.

Finnish engineer Fredrik Idestam started a wood-pulp mill on the banks of the river Nokia and found great success making toilet paper, then expanded to manufacturing rubber boots and generating electricity. In 1981, that same company, Nokia, invented the world's first multinational cellular network, and today it is the largest mobile phone and digital camera maker.

Technology powerhouse Wipro started as a shortening business in India, which then through fits and starts entered the soap business and even made hydraulic cylinders. Azim Premji eventually converted Wipro into a $5 billion IT company, and his personal net worth today is approximately $17 billion.

Try and Try Again

Charles Schwab's first half dozen ventures didn't reach his high hopes. But finally he created a discount brokerage business that was such a hit that it was acquired in the 1980s by Bank of America, which at the time was the world's largest bank. Unfortunately, that deal didn't generate the business that everyone imagined, so Schwab stretched to buy his company back a few years later for more than *four times* the price for which he sold it!

To reduce his debt in the leveraged buyback, he took Schwab public on the New York Stock Exchange, but just weeks before the Great Crash of 1987. The stock fell by more than 70 percent in a day and didn't recover to its initial public offering (IPO) price for about five years.

Success Against All Odds

Chuck Schwab credits his perseverance to parents who witnessed the Great Depression. They cultivated his ambitions to help millions of people achieve their own financial independence. Despite tough times, great families launch many leaders like Schwab, but not as often as you would hope. Many of the great ones had neither the timing nor the families to give them a good start.

Major General Gale Pollock's earliest memories are of her dad threatening her with guns and knives. She was eleven when she confronted her alcoholic father. "Men don't hurt women and daddies don't hurt their daughters!" she declared, facing up to him and choking back tears. Every moment of truth for this woman has been a conscious choice to change things for the better. As a young teen, Pollock's mentor—who had encouraged her during her dangerous early days with her dad—came back from Vietnam with his legs blown off. She was devastated, but turned that anger into action. She signed up as an Army nurse who would later become the first woman to lead the Army medical system.

When controversy broke in 2007 about the quality of health care in military hospitals, she was recruited to jump on that grenade as surgeon general, with a high possibility that she would fail and her career would be destroyed. She took heavy fire, but she turned the legacy of the Army hospitals around.

Character and Competence

What do the people we've described here have in common? Leadership.

To be successful as a leader, you need a combination of two ingredients: character and competence. You need to be a person of integrity. Someone people trust and are willing to follow.

To be trusted in business, you must be *trustworthy*. You must believe in yourself, your company, the essential goodness of your products and services, and in your people. You need to believe that you are offering an excellent product or service in every way, one that makes a difference in the lives of your customers. You must lead by example and inspire others to join you in the exciting project of building a great company.

At the same time, you must become excellent at the key capabilities and functions of leadership and set yourself on a course of continuous improvement throughout your career.

"You need the humility to remind yourself that you've got to get better at everything you do," insisted Amazon founder, Jeff Bezos, when we spoke with him. "I don't know about you, but I'm never done growing my company or myself."

Level 5 Leadership

Management guru Jim Collins uses the phrase "level 5 leadership" to describe the characteristic of the best leaders, those who build great companies. The most fascinating and distinguishing characteristic of level 5 is an often misunderstood trait: *humility*.

As it happens, humility doesn't actually mean being humble. People who are crazy enough to launch businesses as the economy is falling apart and then fight Goliath-size adversaries, are not exactly humble. Humility simply means you have a "burning, driving, relentless ambition to serve and to win," Collins told me, "without the arrogance to delude yourself into believing that you are all knowing or always right."

As a level 5 leader, you don't believe you are perfect. You're just convinced that you have what it takes to succeed and that you can get *better*. You are always looking for new ways to take your game to the next level.

You Can Always Get Better

Bezos's belief that he could create a new type of "virtual" retail store with a mission so massive as to justify the wildly optimistic metaphor of "Amazon" as his company's name was anything but humble! Yet he had the humility to craft a business plan that focused on the fundamentals of leadership in customer service at a time when it was unpopular and at odds with his dot-com era competitors.

While other Internet companies expanded at the speed of light, Amazon's obsession with organizing its products and getting its services working better than anyone else's ironically resulted in complaints about "slower" growth and unprofitability. When the dot-com bubble burst, Amazon survived and prospered while others imploded. After five years of losses, Bezos produced his first profit. This type of humility, combined with the discipline to commit yourself to continuous personal and organizational improvement, is what gives you the "winning edge" in your position and enables your company to outperform your competition.

Would you have imagined that an online company would be among the top 25 companies in customer service, on the same list with a company like the Ritz-Carlton, which has physical places and people to meet and greet you in person? *Business-Week* and J. D. Powers once again lauded Amazon on their list of Customer Service Champs in 2010.

As we'll discuss extensively in this book, the key to winning customers and building businesses has to do with exceeding expectations in comparison with the other alternatives out there. This requires leadership at all levels. Amazon knows how to compete for consumers, and even during the Great Recession, Amazon's net sales soared 28 percent to more than $24 billion in 2009, and net profits jumped 40 percent to nearly a billion dollars.

Nobody Does It Alone

No one does anything worthwhile entirely by themselves. As the leader, your job is to get results through others. One of the best ways to get the most out of your people is to treat them like volunteers, as if they were working for you voluntarily—because they are! Just because you pay them doesn't mean that your best people have to work for you. They are *free agents* who could go elsewhere, and often do.

Since every person is different in some way (often in many ways), the very best leaders have the greatest flexibility in their styles of working with other people. Some people respond best to praise; others need different incentives to get things done. Your ability to get the very best out of the people who report to you is a key measure of your effectiveness as a leader.

The Three P's of Leadership

Three principles are essential to understanding yourself and each member of your team. Most important, they are the key to peak performance.

1. **Purpose: Why does what you do matter to others?** Why exactly do you do what you do? Why do you get up in the morning and work at this job, in this company or industry, producing this particular product or service for this particular type of customer? Your purpose defines how you want to help or improve the life or work of your customer.

2. **Passion: What turns you on?** This question gets to the emotional side of what you do. It is all about what matters to you. While purpose relates to how people view their role in serving others, passion arises when you are doing what you love to do. When you are working at the right job for you, you experience a continuous flow of energy. You like doing your work and learning more about it. You like to talk about your work with others and admire the people who are the best in your chosen field.

Imagine that you were financially independent and you had no limitations on what you could do, be, or have. What would you choose to do even if you weren't getting paid for it? Your answer will often point you toward your passion.

3. **Performance: Goals come last.** Performance is all about breaking down your dreams into actionable steps for which you hold yourself and your team accountable every day. This is where purpose and passion intersect to get things done. As we learned in our World Success Survey for *Success Built to Last,* the challenge is to find a balance between your perception of what you must do for the world—your purpose—and your own passions. When you've found those two things, then it is time to create goals and keep score.

Bad goals happen to good people when they set goals too early. Only after you've found something that matters to other people, *and* something that you love to do, can you be successful at achieving your goals over the long haul.

A Billion Dollars Blowing in the Wind

Aloys Wobben founded German windmill manufacturer Enercon twenty-five years ago, humbly building his first wind turbine in his backyard. He loved tinkering with things like that, and his inspiration came from growing up near the breezy Baltic. He hoped that someday his invention would also be useful to other people. When his passion produced a machine that worked and he found a market that loved it, he set goals and plans to build a great business.

Today, Enercon is the world's fourth-largest windmill producer, with 14 percent market share and turbines deployed in thirty countries. Wobben is now also worth $3.5 billion, but that hasn't changed his geeky interest in building turbines. There's no way he's giving up his first love—his passion for engineering. But what has made him so successful in business is that he feels that he can use that passion to *change the world*.

Wobben's story illustrates what we mean by the three P's of leadership. Wobben is driven by a sense of purpose: He is on a mission to power the world. In addition, he's found other people who share that sense of importance and urgency in doing this work. Wind turbines are *his* passion and *theirs*. He might be happy to do it alone in his garage, but it's even more fun working with like-minded experts who feel that way too. With both purpose and passion working in harmony, he has been able to recruit equally impassioned people who share his vision for creating a high-performance, world-class company.

Doing What You Love

What do you love to do? What parts of your job give you the greatest sense of satisfaction and pleasure, especially when you do them well? If you could choose any job at all, what would it be? How would it be different from what you are doing today?

Chuck Schwab loved entrepreneurship and investing from the time he was thirteen years old, but he still built several businesses that didn't work out for him. Lasting success came only when he combined his personal passion for investing with his talent for making things simple. He struggled with dyslexia and coped with his challenge by breaking things down into fewer, less complex concepts. In so doing, he found a real purpose that mattered to *other* people—making investing easier, cheaper, and simpler for the average investor.

Steve Jobs is famous for starting off by building computers in his garage. His mission was to put a computer on everyone's desk. That was a grand purpose. But it wasn't enough to keep him from dropping out of college to take up calligraphy and fulfill his passion for art and aesthetics. It was only when he combined his personal passion for design with a purpose—creating easy-to-use computers that could "change the world"—that Apple was born.

Having It All

All leaders have to set priorities. Every day is filled with either/or choices. But when it comes to the three P's, successful people choose to do all three rather than just one.

You perform at your best when you align your personal passions with your purpose at work. Think about it: There are many different things you could do for others, and you have many personal interests. The key is to find where your favorite cause intersects with your favorite passion. When you do that, you won't have a problem converting that experience into great performance. And when you can find other people for your team whose purpose, passion, and performance match the job, they become unstoppable.

So ask yourself: Do you know the three P's for your employees?

To build excitement and enthusiasm in others, you must show how excited and enthusiastic you are personally. Show people you are committed to your goals and to the success of the business. Make sure that everyone on your team is empowered to perform beyond their previous levels of accomplishment.

Dedicate yourself to your coworkers' passions and your company's purpose. Inspire loyalty in others by being loyal to your people and to your business. Build courage and confidence in others by giving continuous encouragement and positive reinforcement.

The adage is true: The best leaders are often ordinary people who do extraordinary things. Great leaders elicit extraordinary performance from ordinary people by tapping into their sense of purpose and their passions. Your ability to bring together a group of people and form them into a high-performance team is the single most important quality you can develop for maximum results and continuous personal and professional growth.

Leaders Are Made, Not Born

Peter Drucker wrote, "There may be natural-born leaders, but there are so few of them that they make no difference in the greater scheme of things."

Leaders are self-developed; they work on self-improvement continually. In his book, *Talent Is Overrated*, Fortune writer Geoffrey Colvin shows how most business leaders, at the beginning of their careers, did not demonstrate superb talents and abilities. But over the years, they dedicated themselves to hours and hours of "deliberate practice," identifying the essential skills they would need in order to bring all their other skills to a higher level. They assembled these key skills, one at a time, like parts of a mosaic, until they moved far beyond their coworkers and colleagues.

Success, in the long term, is not an accident. Leaders engage in a continuous, ongoing process of learning by study and practice. In our World Success Survey of leaders in 110 nations, we heard from the most accomplished people that they "learn more from their failures than they do their successes."

You've invested time, effort, money, and your reputation in your business—now harvest the full return on your investment. Keep asking, "What can I learn from this problem or situation?" Don't waste your mistakes.

"Setbacks are not failure, they're feedback. It's data," said Bill Gates.

Harvest Your Weakness

"Nobody has made more mistakes than I have," Ingvar Kamprad, IKEA's founder, admitted to us when we interviewed him. He is a self-described "farm boy" from northern Sweden who created the discount furniture giant and became one of the world's ten richest people. Like Schwab and other high-profile entrepreneurs, Kamprad has dyslexia, and he thinks the challenges he experienced have given him more empathy as a leader.

Most people would consider learning disabilities a weakness or handicap. But great leaders turn their wounds into wisdom. They use every ounce of their uniqueness—the good, the bad, and the ugly—to get things done. Kamprad believes his struggles made him stronger and more committed to making things simple and accessible to the common person. Overcoming what others perceive as a weakness, and turning it into a strength, is a talent worth harvesting.

The point is that you have to be learning from other people all the time so that you can correct what doesn't work. "I've got 100,000 people working for me because I've made so many mistakes," Kamprad joked with us, then became dead serious: "Your job is to make things better by getting better at your job."

Give Credit and Take Responsibility

"You don't need a title to lead; what you need is to be accountable," Kamprad said.

"When something goes wrong, everybody looks to blame everybody else. It's not my fault," Kamprad insisted, pointing at the people on either side of him with an accusing frown. "That's why there needs to be one person who takes responsibility."

The leader's job is to give credit and take responsibility. This means no blame and no excuses. This means that when things go right, you give credit to the people who made it possible. When things go wrong, you as the leader take responsibility. You make the tough decisions, rally the team, and get everyone working toward a common goal. Your ability to achieve this sense of common purpose and commitment is the key measure of your effectiveness.

Oliver Wendell Holmes once noted that there are three kinds of people. First, there are the small few, perhaps 5 percent of us, who make things happen. Second, there is a larger group, perhaps 10 percent to 15 percent of the population, who watch what is happening. The third group is the vast majority, perhaps 80 percent, who have no idea what is happening.

The true leader falls into the first category. Instead of making excuses, you make progress. When you swing into action, you develop the ability to elicit extraordinary performance from ordinary people.

Maintain an Action Orientation

Perhaps the most outwardly identifiable quality of a leader and a top performer is intense action orientation. A leader is in constant motion. The leader is *proactive*, always thinking in terms of what can be done to achieve more and better results, fully aware that most things don't work the first time or often the first several times.

Julie Andrews said, "Success to me is failing nineteen times and succeeding on the twentieth try."

Leadership is action, not position. It's about constant improvement. Leadership is what you *do*, rather than what you wish, hope, say, or intend to do. When you act like a leader in any situation, you become a leader as a result of your behavior.

Unleash Your Energy

When Frances Hesselbein took the helm at the Girl Scouts, the organization was in turmoil. She led a turnaround that won her the Presidential Medal of Freedom and accolades from Peter Drucker, who said, "Frances Hesselbein is the best CEO in America—not just of a nonprofit, but of *any* organization." She founded, with Drucker, the Leader to Leader Institute, where she is president and CEO today.

"It's not about creating enthusiasm, it's about *releasing it*— tapping the incredible energy that people have in their hearts and minds to serve others. There is no force more powerful," Hesselbein said.

When the Girls Scouts were facing serious challenges, she needed to take action, but "command and control" alone would alienate the volunteers. She had to unleash the power within the organization.

The big question she asked was: "When our three million members look at us, can they find *themselves*? We needed to learn more about the children and 650,000 men and women who volunteered. We needed to listen and assess, and most important, every team in every council had to 'own' the outcomes," Hesselbein insisted.

Show Them Why It Matters

"When a girl opens her [Girl Scouts] handbook, she has to be able to find herself," Hesselbein explained, "but our leadership team didn't look like our customer. We found that not all cultures think about daughters the same way. In the Hispanic community, you don't talk directly to the child; you speak to the parents about how this [experience] will build their daughter's character. In the African-American culture, you acknowledge a great legacy of service." For every community you serve, the greatest success comes when you take the effort and have the humility to understand how best to serve that customer.

But here's an important distinction: "You might have to tell people to suck the egg," said Major General (Ret.) Gale Pollock, the first woman to serve as surgeon general of the U.S. Army. "You don't have to tell them how. If you order people to do something that they don't understand, they won't give it all they've got. The greatest performances and courage come when you show them why it matters," she said. "I've been amazed at how people will solve problems when you set the general direction but let them use their creativity to get it done—often much better than I would have ever imagined."

The General pointed her finger: "As a leader, just be clear about what must be done and what's in it for them."

Clarity Is Power

Fully 80 percent of your success in business and in life is going to be determined by your level of clarity in each area. Effective leaders know exactly what they are trying to accomplish. Everyone who reports to them is clear about what they are expected to do to achieve the overall goal. Ineffective leaders are unclear about their responsibilities and, as a result, the people below them and around them are as unclear as well. This leads to enormous amounts of wasted time and effort.

In times of rapid change, there are two great questions for you to ask and answer, over and over again.

The first question is, *What am I trying to do?*

Think on paper. Take the time to sit down and work out exactly what results you are trying to achieve. Be as specific as possible. Most important, create a number or a *measure* against which you can compare your performance to determine whether you are successful in achieving your goals. You've heard it said that "what gets measured gets done." In leadership, "If you can't measure it, you can't manage it."

Measure What You Manage

Many people avoid placing specific measures, benchmarks, and metrics on performance and results because the visibility and accountability are uncomfortable. The unconscious thinking is that if there are no measures, it is not possible to fail and to be judged incompetent or inadequate by the people around you.

But this is not what leaders do. With every decision you make in answering the question, "What am I trying to do?" you must create a measure and set a deadline. You must hold your own feet to the fire, and then hold your team accountable, too.

Almost every business decision costs money. The goal is to spend a specific amount of money to achieve a specific return on investment. It is astonishing to see how many businesses and businesspeople commit resources without asking, "How will we measure whether this expenditure of time, money, and resources has been successful?"

Very often, when you force yourself to do an assessment of what you are trying to do and how you will measure success, you quickly realize that "you can't get there from here." There is no way that you can earn the expected rate of return from the investment, or perhaps there is no way that you can measure it. In either case, you are in danger of wasting precious time and resources.

Continually Reevaluate What You Are Doing

The second big question you ask is, *How am I trying to do it?*

What specific steps, processes, or methodology are you going to use to get from where you are to where you want to go? Is your method working for you? Are you making progress? Or could there be a better way than the method you are using today?

Whenever you experience frustration and obstacles in achieving the goals you have set for yourself and your business, you should be prepared to pull back and call a "time-out."

Napoleon Hill once wrote, "The biggest reason for failure is the inability to make new plans to replace the plans that didn't work."

The fact is that most things don't work, at least at the beginning. You may have to try many different approaches before you find the right combination of activities that enables you to succeed in generating the sales and profitability your business depends upon. As Henry Ford said, "Failure is merely an opportunity to more intelligently begin again."

The Power of Flexibility

One of the most important leadership qualities is that of flexibility. This is as true for you as an individual as it is for your business. The more flexible you are, the more you remain open-minded regarding the various ways that a sales or business goal can be achieved.

The best way to ensure that you remain flexible is to continually ask yourself, "Is there anything I am doing today that, knowing what I now know, I wouldn't start up again if I had it to do over?"

If your answer is, "No, I wouldn't do it again," then your next question is: "How do I change the situation or get out of it, and how fast?" You should be prepared to ask these questions whenever you experience resistance of any kind, in any area.

Clarity About the Goal; Flexibility About the Process

The key to success is to be clear about your goal but be flexible about the process of achieving it. Remember, there is no such thing as failure; there is only *feedback*. Keep your ego out of the situation. Be prepared to abandon any decision you have made in the past if you get new information. Make it clear to the people around you that it is the ultimate result that you care about more than anything else. You are always more concerned with *what's right* rather than with *who's right*.

As a leader, you will ultimately be judged by your ability to get the results that are expected of you. As Phil Knight, founder of Nike, once said, "You only have to be successful the last time."

A Sense of Mission

Most long-lasting leaders think of their work as their mission. They have an overarching vision of something greater and bigger that is beyond and outside of themselves.

Seven Questions for Leaders

It is in difficult markets that the most successful, long-lasting companies invest more, not less, in seven key practices. These principles for sustainable business success are presented here as questions that you must ask yourself:

1. *Your Leadership.* What results are expected of you, and what do your people need from you to contribute their full potential to your business?

2. *Your Plan.* What is your plan to generate greater sales and profitability, and how is it working? Could there be a better way?

3. *Your Team.* How do you attract and keep great people and inspire them to perform at their best in achieving business results?

4. *Your Product.* What are you great at building, who are your ideal customers, and what product or service qualities will attract more of them?

5. *Your Marketing.* What is your competitive advantage— that factor that makes your product or service superior to anything else available, and how do you convey this message to your potential customers?

6. *Your Sales.* What must your potential customers be convinced of so that they want to buy from you rather than your competitor?

7. *Your Customer Experience.* What do your customers need and want, and what can you do to make them so happy that they buy from you again and eagerly tell their friends about your business?

On Capitol Hill, Senator John McCain sighed and leaned on his desk. "As a cocky jet jockey I thought all glory was self-glory," he told us. But when he was shot down during the Vietnam War and endured years of torture, his worldview changed.

"I realized that people want—they really need—to be a part of something greater than themselves," he said. "The buck stops with you. As you become a leader, you see how much that matters to you and how it excites and inspires other people."

Commit to Excellence

In business, perhaps the best vision or mission you can have is to "be the best" at what you do. There is no vision that is more inspiring to more people than to be working for a business whose leader is completely dedicated to excellence, to being the best in that particular market.

Throughout this book are examples of how the key to building a great business is this *commitment to excellence*. It's about a relentless determination to offer products and services that are unmatched in quality by your competitors and treating your customers in such a way that they buy from you again and again.

A visionary goal of being the best in your market unifies and inspires your people. A "shared vision" of excellent performance instills a sense of ownership in each person. And the more opportunity that people have to develop and shape the vision for the future of your business, the more committed they will be to carrying out their responsibilities in the fulfillment of that vision.

A compelling vision that everyone *owns* will motivate them to be a more cohesive, capable, high-spirited team that shows up earlier, works harder, and stays later. This kind of goal gives each person on the team a clear sense of purpose and direction and makes working *with you* and *for you* a source of inspiration and fulfillment.

Imagine No Limitations

What is your vision for yourself and your business in the months and years ahead? What words would you use to describe your perfect company one year from today? Imagine there are no boundaries in what you can accomplish with your organization. Imagine that you could wave a magic wand over your future and create your business so that it was perfect in every respect. What would it look like?

Imagine that you could create and offer the best products and services possible for your market. How would you describe them? How would your customers describe them? And most important, what could you start doing today to make that vision of product and service excellence a reality sometime in the future?

If your business was perfect in every way, how would it be *different* from today? Einstein wrote, "Your imagination is your preview of life's coming attractions."

Leaders have an exciting picture of where they want to lead their organizations. They share this vision with everyone around them, and continually encourage and welcome ideas and suggestions to help make that vision a reality.

Invest in the Future

One of your chief responsibilities as a leader is to think about the future. Only the leader is ultimately tasked with this responsibility. Leaders are continually thinking through and planning their next moves, and evaluating the consequences of those moves. That's why you need to spend the time to create a compelling and clear vision. Only then can you grasp the "big picture."

Leaders engage in *teleological* thinking, projecting into the future. Before acting, you should consider all the possible consequences of a decision. Develop alternative courses of action in case the first choice does not work out. Have a Plan B ready if Plan A is not successful.

As a leader, keep focused on the desired results so that when you think through the various scenarios—those things that could go right or could go wrong—you remain flexible about the various ways of achieving the outcome you are after.

Focus on Results

One of the most important questions leaders ask of themselves is, "What *results* are expected of me? Why am I on the payroll?"

To keep focused on the most important results he can achieve, a leader must also ask: "What can I, and only I do that, if done well, will make a real contribution to my organization?"

The entire business of business and of life is the setting of priorities. You know the saying: "Leaders determine what is to be done; managers determine the best way to do it."

In setting priorities, the job of the leader is to determine the "sequence of events." What gets done first? What has to be done second? And what is not to be done at all? In business, there is always the *law of the excluded alternative*. This law says that "doing one thing means not doing something else."

The Myth of Multitasking

Studies by Professor Cliff Nass at Stanford University in 2010 again confirmed that even exceptionally bright young people who appear to be experts at multitasking among e-mail, instant messaging, and live communication are not as accurate or effective in doing work as those who do one thing at a time. As a leader, you obviously have too much to do at any given time. But it turns out that you are smartest when you focus on one task right now. Your effectiveness as a leader is largely determined by what you choose to do, and what you choose not to do, at any given moment.

If you make a list of tasks that you have to accomplish, the 80/20 rule will apply. Twenty percent of your tasks will eventually account for 80 percent of your results. Sometimes it is the 90/10 rule. Sometimes in a list of ten tasks that you may accomplish, one of the tasks will be worth more than all the others put together.

Your ability as a leader to focus intensely on the most important results expected of you largely determines your success or failure in your position. When you discipline yourself to work single-mindedly on your most important tasks, you will accomplish two or three times as much as the average person. This is why all top leaders are described as being "intensely result-oriented."

Leaders Develop High Self-Esteem

Your focus on results as a leader helps you develop a positive self-image. Self-esteem is defined as "how much you like yourself." The better your self-concept, the better you do your work. An important element of self-esteem is called *self-efficacy*. This is a feeling of competence. It means that you are good at what you do and capable of achieving the goals and results that you have set for yourself. You feel competent and capable at what you are doing and you are eager to do more of it.

"The way you *feel* about yourself has everything to do with how you perform as an individual in your own work and as a manager of people," said Steve Rodgers, President and Owner of Windermere Properties and former CEO of Prudential Bache California Realty, a division of Warren Buffett's company, Berkshire Hathaway. "When the real estate crash hit, you could instantly see the difference in managers who believed in themselves. It's what separated those who were resilient in the tough times from those who couldn't recover from adversity and rebuild their objectives," he observed.

Turn Your Inside Out

You always perform on the *outside* consistent with the beliefs and ideas you have about yourself on the *inside*. To change and improve in performance and effectiveness, you must begin by changing your self-concept and the self-concepts of others.

Leaders with high self-esteem and positive self-images are more sensitive to people and situations. They are much more perceptive and aware of what is going on around them. The reason is simple: Because they are not wrestling with their own feelings of inferiority or inadequacy, they can see the world around them with greater calmness and clarity.

William Glasser, the psychologist, described what he called the "fully functioning person (FFP)" as someone who is completely nondefensive. This means that the more you like and respect yourself, and are comfortable with yourself, the less defensive you feel. You have no need to defend or explain away a mistake or problem. Instead, you deal with it candidly and directly. This type of nondefensiveness disarms other people and defuses tense situations.

Be Honest with Yourself

When leaders are honest with themselves, they readily admit that they have both strengths and weaknesses. Leaders organize their work to maximize their strengths and minimize their weaknesses. To make your maximum contribution, you should focus on getting better and better at the few things in which you excel, and delegate the rest to others who can do those things better and easier than you can.

Perhaps the most admirable outward quality of a leader is "authenticity." You express this quality when you honestly admit that you are not perfect. Only a person with high self-esteem can allow himself to be vulnerable. This quality, however, makes people want to work with you and help you.

This is not the same as whining or weeping about your insecurities or someone else's. It is simply being honest with others, admitting mistakes, and remaining open to input and ideas from others.

How You Treat Others

When Sir Richard Branson of Virgin Brands experimented with a television series based on *The Apprentice,* he disguised himself as a limo driver and watched keenly how he was treated by the entrepreneur he was testing. Those who treated "the help" poorly were "fired" from the show. As Thomas Carlyle wrote, "You can tell a big man by the way he treats little men."

To be an effective leader, you should be the same with everyone, the weak and the powerful alike. The true leader is as genuine and friendly with a pilot as with a flight attendant.

Great Leaders Are Change Agents

"There is a myth that people hate change. Not true!" said Ford CEO Alan Mulally, rather insistently, when we interviewed him. "What scares them isn't change, it's uncertainty. They worry about whether the changes are good or bad. People love change when it involves pleasant surprises," he winked. "What they fear are the unpleasant ones."

Mulally can see change happening all around him in the automotive business, and he is fiercely committed to driving it.

From Mulally's spacious but sparse corner office in Dearborn, with its floor-to-ceiling windows, you can see Chrysler and GM headquarters. "I can keep an eye on 'em," he smiled mischievously. But that's not really where Ford's effervescent CEO focuses his attention. He knows his neighboring automakers aren't the problem.

When Mulally joined Ford Motor Company in 2006, however, the company looked like it was in the worst shape of the Big Three. Mulally insisted on borrowing almost $24 billion to float the company through the recession. But more important, he intended to spend billions of those dollars on making Ford's products great again for customers.

Turning a Profit

Ford still lost more than $14 billion in 2008 and wasn't expecting a profit until 2011. But Mulally's relentless focus delivered the company's first profit a year early, at the beginning of 2010, and the stock soared by *sevenfold* from its low. The company became No. 1 among the U.S. automakers, and the press gave Ford awards for best car and truck of the year.

What is unique about Mulally is that he's the first fellow to run Ford who isn't a *car guy*. He's more of a rocket scientist. He's a meticulous engineer who led Boeing's renaissance with a new aircraft, the innovative 777, that saved his previous employer. When Airbus in Europe leaped past Boeing's long dominance in the aircraft market, Mulally used his deep expertise, attention to quality, and passion for listening to help Boeing reconnect with customers. Boeing came roaring back to No. 1 in global market share.

"You've got to understand and care deeply about what your product is doing for people," he says. Mulally's passion for engineering is exceeded only by his evangelical insistence that "you find a way to delight customers at every point of contact."

Getting Back in Touch with Buyers

Mulally is transforming what had become a stodgy, out-of-touch image for Ford and investing in "super-cool high-tech" and "awesomely great quality," as Mulally puts it, sounding like an excited teenager. And, just as Henry Ford did at the beginning of the twentieth century, Mulally is making these "hip" features available not just on Ford's most expensive brands, but on smaller, cheaper cars that are accessible to anyone, like the new subcompact, the Ford Focus.

Focus, Focus, Focus

Focus is a perfect metaphor for what Mulally has done with Ford, and it's a mandate for what you must do as a leader. Your job is to boil down all the moving parts to the few things that really matter.

"You've got to *focus, focus, focus!*" Mulally said, punctuating each word with three slaps on the back. He has focused Ford on less than twenty brands, instead of ninety-seven. "Good grief, how helpful is it to customers to show them a hundred different brands?" he said. "And how could we be any good at doing that?"

When you meet him, you'll get a warm handshake, or even a hug and a hand on your shoulder. Most important, he'll listen more intensely to what you say than a family member would.

Send him an e-mail today and chances are you'll actually get one back.

Here's the key: Mulally doesn't love cars; he loves customers and *great* cars. "And to build well-engineered cars that people want to buy, you've got to have exciting products and services that are built to last," he gushed. "You can only do that by being a great listener."

Leaders Are Listeners

The best leaders spend 50 percent or more of their time listening carefully. They dominate the listening and let the other person dominate the talking. As a leader, you listen with undivided attention.

When was the last time you actually listened single-mindedly to one of your staff members or managers? Can you remember when you last listened to someone without interruptions or distractions from either telephone calls or drop-in visitors, when you just focused intently on the person speaking with you, ignoring all else?

When Mulally arrived at Ford, he used a technique he had refined at Boeing. He found a way to instantly shift the senior executives on his team from talkers to listeners by changing the way he evaluated his team's performance. "It always comes down to incentives. What's the incentive for someone to behave differently? Is it recognition, time, or more money? No. It's usually *visibility*," he said.

"When you give a speech, you'll be scored by the audience," he told his team. "So those executives who were smart enough to leave lots of time for Q & A got better grades than those who lectured. And those managers who encouraged . . . a dialogue with the team came out on top."

Great leaders encourage input and change, and the best way

to measure them is based on feedback they get from their best people. You are going to give the best scores to leaders you trust and to leaders who listen.

The Essential Quality of Leadership

How do you build trust? By meeting or exceeding expectations. By saying what you'll do and then doing what you say. Integrity is perhaps the most valued and respected quality of leadership.

Do you stand up and speak out for what you believe? Do you demonstrate the courage to stay the course when the going gets tough and the outcome looks uncertain?

It is the leader's job to stay calm and in control, especially when everyone around you is wondering whether it's the right decision or if it was a mistake to commit to a particular course of action. When you exude confidence in yourself, in the decision, and in the people around you, you instill the same feelings and attitudes in others.

Leaders have what is called "courageous patience." Between the decision and the result, there is always a period of uncertainty when no one knows if the effort is going to be successful. If you have lived with this feeling many times in your career, you're in good company. So has Alan Mulally, and anyone who has the courage of his convictions.

The Future Belongs to Risk Takers

The future belongs to those who are willing to take calculated risks to move forward. As a leader, your role is to carefully gather all the information possible about a particular decision or commitment of resources, and then take the initiative. Winston Churchill wrote, "Courage is rightly considered the foremost of the virtues, for upon it, all others depend."

Perhaps the biggest single obstacle to success in life is the *fear of failure.* Many people are so concerned with the possibility of failing that they play it safe and hold themselves back from taking any chances at all.

The leader is different. One of the qualities of courage is *boldness.* Boldness is the willingness to initiate action in the face of uncertainty and possible failure. As the leader you must be willing to take action with no guarantees of success and a substantial likelihood of failure, at least in the short term. The leader practices the Wayne Gretzky philosophy: "You miss every shot you don't take."

The next chapter shows you how to take that courage and creativity and turn them into an action plan that works for you and your company in any market.

CHAPTER 1 CHECKLIST TO BECOME A GREAT LEADER

1. What three **accomplishments** as a leader are you most proud of?

    a. _____

    b. _____

    c. _____

2. What are your most **useful and informative failures,** and how are you harvesting them for your business?

    a. _____

    b. _____

    c. _____

3. How do you demonstrate to others the **courage** to stay the course when the going gets tough and the outcome looks uncertain?

    a. _____

    b. _____

    c. _____

4. What are the most important measures you use to determine **how effective you are** as a leader? Why are you on the payroll?

    a. _____

    b. _____

    c. _____

5. Is there anything that you are doing today that, knowing what you now know, you wouldn't start up again if you had it to do over? **What can you stop doing** as a leader today?

    a. _____

    b. _____

    c. _____

6. What are the three P's—the **purpose, passion, and performance**—of your employees, your best customers, and your family?

    a. _____

    b. _____

    c. _____

7. If your leadership and work situation were perfect in every way, **how would it be different** from today?

   a. _____

   b. _____

   c. _____

What **one action** are you going to take immediately as the result of your answers to the previous seven questions?

_____

_____

_____

Develop a Great Business Plan

"You decide what it is you want to accomplish and
then you lay out your plans to get there, and then
you just do it. It's pretty straightforward."

—NANCY DITZ, MARATHONER

Peeople and organizations with clear visions, values, and
plans tend to accomplish far more and do it faster than
their competitors. When everyone in your organization is
united by a clear strategic vision of your desired future state,
you create a powerful mental synergy that will move you toward
your goals and move your goals toward you.

The major reasons for success in business and in life are
focus and concentration. The major reasons for failure are lack

of direction and diffusion of effort. This chapter shows you how to achieve far more of the former and avoid much of the latter.

Alexander the Great

The world has become an increasingly challenging place for businesspeople. Not only is it more difficult than ever to create a business, but there are more threats from competitors, angry consumers, and government regulators. In the battleground we are facing in the new century, it's helpful to look to history for insight.

Alexander the Great was an extraordinarily gifted strategic planner in his military conquests. Had he been alive today, he could have taught us much about how to survive and thrive in turbulent economic times. More than two millennia ago, at the Battle of Arbela in 331 BC, he became the master of the known world by defeating Darius of Persia in a pitched battle where Alexander was outnumbered five to one. Alexander was able to accomplish this incredible feat because of his ability to focus his limited strength on the one strategic variable upon which hinged the power of the Persian army: Darius himself.

Whether or not you are a fan of military metaphor, the reality is that the economic situation today is putting many entrepreneurs and managers in survival mode, in constant combat to achieve profitability. You should become familiar with seven key military principles of strategy that are applicable to setting corporate strategy in an uncertain business world today:

1. Objective
2. Offensive
3. Concentration
4. Economy

5. Flexibility

6. Surprise

7. Momentum

The Principle of the Objective

Alexander had a clear vision of what he wanted to accomplish and why. He knew that he would have to achieve a decisive victory over the Persian army to bring all of the Persian empire under his control. He also knew that the Persian army was made up of contingents from all over the empire. The only factor that held them together was loyalty to Darius himself. If Alexander could kill or disable Darius, the rest of the army would break up and scatter.

The night before the battle, Alexander called his officers together and told them how they were going to win the battle the following morning against such overwhelming odds. They would not try to defeat the entire Persian army. There were too many. They would instead focus their army and hurl it like a spear into the center of the Persian line at Darius himself. Then Alexander told his officers to go back to their troops and give them the order of battle. It was simply, "Kill Darius!"

After the battle began, at the appropriate moment, Alexander led his companion cavalry, perhaps the finest cavalry in the world at that time, into the center of the Persian army, straight at Darius. The attack came so suddenly that Darius was completely unprepared. According to historians, Darius leaped onto a mare and rode frantically off the battlefield, leaving his army to fend for itself.

Just as Alexander had predicted, the army soon began to break up and scatter. At the end of the day, he had destroyed the Persian army and become master of the greatest empire in the world. One key lesson from Darius' defeat is that you as a leader cannot abandon your team or neglect your primary objective no matter how sudden or furious the challenge you're experiencing. Your behavior at that key moment has huge influence on your team and on your chances for victory.

The Principle of the Offensive

Even though Alexander was greatly outnumbered by the army of Darius, he initiated the attack and thereby took control of the battle. His actions illustrate what Napoleon said many years later: "No great battles are ever won on the defensive."

Your ability to develop your strategic plan and then to launch it like a javelin into the heart of the market, practicing the "continuous offensive," enables you to take the initiative and control your financial destiny.

The Principle of Concentration

Alexander was able to concentrate his forces on one objective, the Persian king Darius. In business, your ability to concentrate your limited resources on selling the very best products and services you offer to the very best potential prospects for those products and services is the key to business victory.

The Principle of Economy

Alexander used his outnumbered forces to accomplish the objective with the least expenditure of men and resources. By the end of the day, the Persian army was eliminated as a fighting force while the casualties to Alexander's army were minor.

In strategic thinking, your goal is to use brain power and

creativity to achieve your goals of market success with the minimum possible expenditure of time and money.

The Principle of Flexibility

The greatest talent an organization can acquire is flexibility. Alexander's forces were able to remain flexible and shift the direction of attack when the opportunity arose. Each officer on the field had the authority to act in response to changing conditions. In the Persian army, Darius was the supreme commander. Each officer was assigned to perform a specific function without deviation or diversion. When the battle unfolded in an unexpected way, the Persian army was unable to adapt fast enough.

In business, with turbulence, uncertainty, and change taking place incessantly, unpredictably, and unexpectedly, you must maintain the flexibility to change your product/service mix, people and assignments, markets and sales techniques, products and prices, and every other factor of your business to achieve sales and profitability against determined competition.

The Principle of Surprise

Alexander used surprise to his great advantage. Instead of lining up his Macedonian soldiers in a long row to confront the Persian army, making it easy for the Persians to overlap the Macedonians on the flanks, Alexander organized his army in a more flexible formation, which allowed him to shift his point of attack and forces as the battle unfolded.

In your business, you must be prepared to do the unexpected, to counter your competition with rapid changes in products, prices, promotional methods, and places of sale. You must always think of doing something that your competition has not anticipated.

The Principle of Momentum

Once Alexander achieved his desired objective by driving Darius from the field, he immediately focused all his forces to exploit his "market advantage" to the fullest extent possible in the shortest period of time, thereby achieving the destruction of the Persian army.

In business, once you have a market advantage, you must "sell all you can." You must seize the day and press forward aggressively to achieve every dollar of profitable sales that you possibly can while the window of opportunity is open and before your competition has a chance to counterattack.

Business coach Marshall Goldsmith says, "There are three factors that must dominate your thinking and which will determine your success or failure: competition, competition, and competition."

The Battle of the Business Plans

With financial markets on the verge of collapse in 2008, Mike Moritz and his partners at Sequoia Capital huddled with business owners to review a *slide deck of doom,* a fifty-six-slide PowerPoint plan describing a brave new world without credit, where nothing would be financed without solid cash flows. They predicted it would take years for the world to recover.

It is difficult to plan for economic scenarios like the one experienced in 2008–2009. Fortunately for Moritz, the dot-com bust a decade earlier had given his team experience in responding to sudden changes in fortune. When the economy imploded, they knew how to shift risk and cut costs faster than ever before.

No successful investor in the world was immune from the pain, and Moritz is one investor who has seen it all. Sequoia has launched many legends in California's Silicon Valley, including Apple, Cisco, Atari, Google, YouTube, Zappos, and Yahoo.

When the storm descended, Moritz and the management teams of his companies undertook a crash course in strategic and financial planning. They worked around the clock to create many different versions of their business plans. Moritz would often reassure those who had pulled all-nighters by repeating an ironic-sounding mantra: *Plans may not work, but planning does!*

In other words, the economy may not make it possible to deliver on your plan exactly as you planned it, but the *process* of planning is mission critical. It is the only way to be clear about your choices. Planning is essential to consider what it takes to survive, grow, and prosper in any economic environment.

In turbulent economic cycles, the planning process is no longer the abstract endeavor taught in business school; every alternative must be considered and the best options turned instantly into action. During the crisis, Moritz's companies had a clear plan to track where every penny was spent and tie it back to customer service, quality, innovation, and growth.

Your ability to develop a great business plan, and then to set and implement business strategy, is at the heart of your business success.

Make the Plan Useful

When we talk about a business plan, we are not referring to that binder or spreadsheet that you worked so hard to produce just to impress someone else, but then never looked at again after your presentation. We are talking about a living document—a guide that you can use to power your business.

"Judging by all the hoopla surrounding business plans, you would think that the only things standing between a would-be entrepreneur and spectacular success are glossy five-color charts, a bundle of meticulous-looking spreadsheets, and a decade of month-by-month financial projections," says William A. Sahlman, professor of business administration at the Harvard Business School. "Nothing could be further from the truth."

You will find entire college courses focusing on business plans that are philosophically correct but practically useless.

Put Measures in Your Plans

What is missing from most plans is that they are disconnected from what actually drives your customers and the success of your business. "In manufacturing, such a driver might be the yield on a production process; in magazine publishing, the anticipated renewal rate; or in software, the impact of using various distribution channels," Professor Sahlman noted. In every business there are a few key measures that make all the difference.

What are the three drivers that impact your profitability most? What three factors drive your customers to buy and remain loyal? Your task is to get clear about those questions.

Practice What You Preach

Effective leaders are clear about the measures they use to monitor the success of their businesses and demonstrate this financial discipline in everything they do.

For example, Warren Buffett's *frugality* is legendary, and it is more than an act or old habit. It's symbolic for his team. Buffett is famous for driving older cars, preferring Diet Coke to expensive wine, and living in his long-time residence in Omaha.

IKEA's discount furniture founder, Ingvar Kamprad, one of the world's ten richest men, rides the public train, lives rather modestly, and constantly challenges his people to make things cheaper *and* more beautiful at the same time. While being interviewed for this book, Kamprad treated Mark to a meal of Swedish meatballs in the cafeteria at an IKEA store in St. Gallen, Switzerland, then drove him back to his motel in a seven-year-old Volvo. Is it a show or is he really frugal? The only thing that matters is that he's sending everyone a message about setting the right priorities in his business.

The world's richest man, according to Forbes, is Carlos Slim Helu. The self-made telecommunications tycoon, whose parents emigrated from Lebanon to Mexico City, has lived in the same house for decades and his master bedroom is famously small. Like Bill Gates and Buffett before him, Carlos Slim would rather not make a fuss about being the world's richest person. He knows that a fickle stock market could change that situation in a heartbeat.

Ironically, the world's wealthiest entrepreneurs recommend that you don't try to keep up with the Joneses or worry about who has the most wealth, power, or status. Instead, their stories show how success is acquired by staying focused on what's really important to the entrepreneur's long-term strategy.

Five Good Reasons for Setting Strategy

Before the "What?" always comes the "Why?" It is only possible for you to set effective strategy and develop a great business plan when you are crystal clear about why you are doing it. There are five reasons for setting business strategy:

1. **To increase return on equity invested.** The first purpose is to organize and reallocate your resources to increase

your return on the amount of money actually invested in your company. It is to earn more bottom-line profitability than you are producing today.

2. **To reposition yourself relative to your competitors.** Business strategy allows you to change customer perceptions and responses to your product or service offerings. You must continually upgrade your existing product and service offerings and develop new ones in response to changing wants, demands, tastes, and customer preferences.

3. **To capitalize on strengths and opportunities.** You must take advantage of those special talents and capabilities that make your business superior to your competition and do things that your competition cannot duplicate, at least in the short term. You must remain open to unexpected changes in your marketplace. Whenever there is an economic disruption or a business reversal, stop the clock and rethink your strategy to make sure it is appropriate to the new situation. Always be open to the possibility that your current strategy is no longer the best for the markets of today and tomorrow.

4. **To form a basis for making better decisions.** All strategic and business thinking must lead to immediate action to increase sales and profitability relative to the past, and relative to your competition.

5. **To attract investors and financing.** Raising capital requires a special approach to the planning process. Look at your business through the eyes of a potential lender or investor, and create plans that make your company an attractive place to invest. The firms that typically receive the most dollars in first-time financings

are in businesses that have at least four things going for them:

- **Great business model.** Your idea should open new, large markets in ways that are tough for competitors to copy quickly. The size and profitability of the market opportunity is critical. That's why you need a great plan to show investors.

- **Scalability.** Can the business build the necessary products and services rapidly and achieve economies of scale with as little capital investment and labor as possible? The less money invested, of course, the lower the risk and the higher the return on investment.

- **Intellectual property (IP).** Do you have patents or other ways to help protect your ideas? Patent protection is no guarantee, but it does improve the chances of building businesses that have more sustainable competitive advantages in the marketplace.

- **Experience in related fields.** Investors highly prize gifted leaders who are "serial entrepreneurs" – business veterans who have experience in other similar ventures or who can become great managers or delegators quickly. Investors are betting on an idea and its execution, not just you. They need to know their investment isn't entirely at risk if the founder is "lost or stolen." You must convince them that your business is a good place to invest and that you are a great manager who can help them profit handsomely. You have to prove to investors that you have the ability to put together a leadership team quickly and grow the company by calling on the skills, efforts, and commitment of leaders other than yourself on the operating staff.

Six Key Questions in Strategic Planning

Whenever you must create or reinvent the direction of your organization, there are six questions, in order, that you must answer correctly. You've heard the expression "garbage in, garbage out." The quality of your thinking and decisions is determined solely by the quality of the information you begin with.

1. **Where are you now? What is your current situation?** If your business was in trouble and you hired an outside consulting firm to come in to help, the first things the consultants would do would be to determine your exact levels of sales in every product/service area, the relative profitability of each of your products and services, the trends in each area, the amount of money you have and will have in the foreseeable future, and your position relative to your competition. These are all pieces of information that you can and must generate for yourself.

2. **How did you get to where you are today?** What were the factors and decisions that led to your current situation? Be your own management consultant. Be prepared to face "the brutal truth," as Jim Collins calls it, about how you got to where you are today. Refuse to flinch or exaggerate, especially when you have problems with sales and profitability.

Jack Welch insisted his managers practice the "reality principle," which he defined as "being willing to face the world as it is, rather than the way you wish it could be."

You cannot resolve a problem or resolve a difficult situation unless you have the courage to face the current facts squarely, whatever they are. Reevaluate all your business activities. Is everything you are doing necessary to win and keep customers? What savings could you generate by partnering with other companies to do work or carry overhead? Could you share a warehouse or manufacturing plant with a neighboring firm? Can you share an accounting department? What activities could you outsource without reducing quality or service to your customers?

3. **Where do you want to go from here?** What do you want to accomplish? Clearly describe the ideal desired outcome for your business. Project forward five years and imagine that your business was perfect. The greater clarity you have about where you want to be at a specific time in the future, the easier it will be for you to create a great business plan, or blueprint, that will enable you to get from where you are today to where you want to go. Be specific about your future goals and desired outcome. For instance:

- How much product would you be selling five years from now?

- How much would you be earning (gross and net), and how does that compare with your competitors?

- How many people would be working in your business?

- Who would your customers be, and where would they be located?

4. **How do you get from where you are today to where you want to be in the future?** What are the steps that you will have to take to create your ideal future business? Make a list. Write down every single thing that you can possibly think of that you would have to do to achieve your goals in the future. As you

Turn a Cost Center into a Profit Center

Amazon's massive online store operation requires large computer centers which are also a huge cost center for the company. Then management began asking, "What if we could turn that competency into a profit center?" As a result, Amazon's massive IT infrastructure has become another business opportunity for the company, with Amazon renting space on its computer servers to other businesses.

Why not trust Amazon, which already maintains massive online networks, to rent IT services to you cheaper than you can do it yourself? Amazon is leveraging a core competency and saving its customers money.

Accenture, the global professional services firm, has helped Best Buy and other Fortune 500 companies save billions of dollars by not only outsourcing but also consolidating the overhead of many administrative and operating functions, including many aspects of HR, IT, and accounting, all into a central service center that shares the same staff, software, and hardware. This approach benefits *many companies* at the same time—even some of Best Buy's competitors! Best Buy can focus more on what it does best, consumer electronics retailing, and offload as much of the other necessary work to firms that can do it for less. Could you do something similar in your own business?

think of new actions, tasks, or steps, add them to the list. This information then becomes your recipe or formula for achieving your business goals.

5. **What obstacles will you have to overcome? What problems will you have to solve?** Of all the problems or obstacles standing between you and your desired future outcomes, what are the biggest or most important? If you aren't *already* a fast-growing, highly profitable company, why not? What is holding you back? What are the critical constraints or limiting factors for growth? Sometimes, just identifying and removing one critical block or obstacle can turn your company into a more profitable enterprise.

6. **What additional knowledge, skills, or resources will you require to achieve your strategic objectives?** What additional competencies or capabilities will you need if you want to lead your field in the years ahead? Every business begins and grows around a set of core competencies, but there are almost always additional core competencies that you'll need to acquire or develop over time. If your company is already the market leader, then explore what new areas you can excel in. And most of all, ask yourself what you can do, starting today, to begin to achieve those core competencies to create your business of the future.

Drucker's Five Questions

Peter Drucker insisted that leaders ponder several deceptively simple questions about their organization. It takes a few seconds to read them and often it takes hours to answer them. The clarity and simplicity of each question forces you to reexamine many assumptions you and your team may have about your organization. Here are the five questions:

1. **What is your mission?** Why does your organization exist in the first place? What are you trying to accomplish for your client?

2. **Who is your customer?** Describe the exact person you are focused on satisfying with your activities.

3. **What does your customer value?** What is it that you do especially well that you are uniquely suited to provide to your customers? How can you exceed the standards set by your competition?

4. **What results are you trying to accomplish?** How do you measure success?

5. **What is your plan?** How do you go about satisfying your customers and getting the results that are most important?

We challenge you to take enough time with your team to get these answers right when you do your planning. Based on your answers to these five questions, you can plan what to do next and what actions to take immediately.

Determining the Corporate Mission

The corporate mission is a clear statement of why the company exists in the first place. The corporate mission states an overarching goal and purpose, based on the values that guide decision making at every level of the company. It should be so clear and simple that, as Drucker also said, "It should fit on a T-shirt."

Ideally, your mission statement should refer to your customer and the difference that your product or service is going to make in the life or work of your customer. YouTube founder Chad Hurley wanted to make it possible for people to send their own homemade videos to anyone. His original mission was a slogan on his website that said simply, BROADCAST YOURSELF.

"Charles Schwab's mission was to be the 'most useful and ethical financial services company.' That statement reflected our vision and our values – it was our way of life!" said business strategist Karen Chang, former President of the Charles Schwab Individual Investor Enterprise.

Larry Page and Sergey Brin founded Google to organize millions of web pages so they could be found instantly and easily. Their original mission was to "index everything." FedEx decided to bring packages to "the world on time," and for a long while its memorable and effective ad slogan was "absolutely, positively overnight."

What is your mission statement? How do you intend to benefit your customer? A mission is something that you can accomplish. You can measure it. A third party can tell you if you have achieved it or not. What is yours?

Your Most Valuable Asset

Within the first five minutes of meeting the legendary marketing scholar, Theodore Levitt, at Harvard Business School, he told Mark: "There is one asset more valuable than any other in your organization and your life – and you need to build it with care and ingenuity at every step in your journey. Your most valuable asset is your reputation." A company's reputation is defined as "how it is known and trusted (or not) by its customers," he said.

If you want people say that you have "a *great* company," then examine your reputation:

■ What is your reputation today? What do people say about your business?

- What would you like your reputation to be? How would you like one customer to describe your company to another customer? How would you like outsiders to describe your products? Your services? Your people? Your management?

- What *should* people be saying about you and your company if you wanted to be the best in your chosen market?

- Most of all, what would have to happen, starting today, for you to create the kind of reputation you desire?

What would you have to do for people to say, "This is a great company!"

Choosing Your Competition

Choosing your strategy means choosing whom you will compete against. Don't delude yourself. You might think you have no competition in your business, but there is always competition for your customer's dollar, even if it's not obvious.

Who are your main competitors today? What companies do your prospects choose to buy from, if not from you? What could you do to offset the perceived advantages of your competitors that cause your potential customers to buy from them?

Who are your secondary competitors? This is an important question because you want to know the other ways your prospective customers spend dollars that they could be spending with you. For example, when Carnival Cruise Lines asked this question during a seminar with Brian, the management team didn't mention other oceangoing cruise lines. Instead, it immediately identifies itself as competing with all other "land-based vacations" and destinations.

Key Players in Setting Strategy

Who should be involved in the strategic planning process? The simple answer is that *everyone* who will be responsible for carrying out a part of the strategic plan should be involved in creating the plan in the first place.

Start with the company owner or the chief executive officer, the president, the chairperson, or whoever is the key person whose agreement, position, or authority is necessary to put the strategic plan into motion. If the plan is not totally supported from the top down, it will be ignored; or worse, it will be sabotaged. Take a look at the incentives or disincentives that people in the company have to implement the new strategy.

Setting corporate strategy is like improving your overall health. You must first put the right incentives in place to make sure that everyone has a vested interest in making the plan successful.

Saving Time and Money with Planning

Developing a complete business plan *before* starting operations will save you enormous amounts of time and money, and many months and years of hard work, frustration, and failure. But don't put your business plan on a shelf. It should be changing constantly with each market test and every experiment to make you better and better.

A clear business plan gives you a competitive advantage. The process of planning—which includes getting continuous feedback on your progress and thinking through every detail—sharpens your mind and awareness, and makes it far more likely that you will be successful.

Finding the Right Way to Measure Your Progress

Ultimately your career and your company will be valued on the basis of key operating and financial metrics. One of your most important challenges as a leader is to find the right measures and focus on them. Every key person in your business must know with complete clarity which numbers are the most important and the most predictive of business success.

All business success is the result of changing one or more of these key numbers. Sometimes, these are called key performance indicators (KPIs) or critical success factors (CSFs).

We offer you this very simple sample set of thirty-three measures to inspire or provoke you to create your own dashboard for your business:

1. Sales of all products from all sources (your top line)

2. Other revenues of all kinds (nonsales activities)

3. Cost of goods sold (all inclusive)

4. Expenses (every cost of doing business)

5. Salaries and wages (usually the biggest single expense)

6. Lead generation (number and cost per lead)

7. Conversion rate from lead to customer

8. Cost of customer acquisition

9. Average size of sale

10. Average gross profit per sale

11. Average gross profit margin as a percentage

12. Average net profit per sale for each product or service

13. Average cost per sale (specific total cost per product)

14. Average number of times a customer buys

15. Lifetime value of a customer

16. Sales per employee (average)

17. Sales per day, week, month, or even hour

18. Sales per specific product or service

19. Average size of up-sells or cross-sells

20. Average number of referrals received

21. Average sales per square foot (retail)

22. ROI (return on money invested and working in the business)

23. ROE (return on owner's equity in the business)

24. ROS (return on sales, or net profit from sales after all expenses)

25. Amount of receivables and how long outstanding

26. Amount of payables and when due

27. Amount of money in the bank

28. Amount of money drawn down on credit lines

29. Amount of debt in total owed by the business

30. General trend of key numbers

31. Number of orders for future fulfillment

32. Number and size of bad debts and past-due payments

33. Daily active users of your website, your services, your products

In addition to these metrics, there are hundreds more for every industry. Select a combination that is best for your unique business, to drive your customers and your team, and use those metrics as your dashboard.

Sometimes, an intense companywide focus on improving one key number can transform your business, but you must know which measure that is. This is a chief responsibility of management. You must develop a plan, a "full-court press," to improve the most important number in your business. What is the most important metric for your organization? Whatever your answer, the dramatic improvement of your "economic denominator" is the key to building a great business.

CHAPTER 2 CHECKLIST TO DEVELOP A GREAT BUSINESS PLAN

Become your own management consultant and save yourself a bundle of time and money. Here's a seven-step process you can follow:

1. What is your **vision** for your business? What problem(s) do you solve for customers? If your business was perfect sometime in the future, what words would you and others use to describe it?

   a. _____

   b. _____

   c. _____

2. What are the three most important **values** that you believe in and stand for and that guide and determine your behaviors and business activities?

   a. _____

   b. _____

   c. _____

3. **Strategic objectives.** What are the *goals* that you must achieve to build a successful business?

   a. What level of *sales* do you want to achieve over the next one, two, three, four, and five years?

   b. What level of *profitability* do you want to achieve from these sales?

   c. What *rate of growth* do you want to achieve in the years ahead?

4. **Tactical objectives.** What are the *activities* that you must engage in to accomplish your strategic objectives?

   a. What specific kind and quality of *products and services* do you intend to produce?

   b. What are your *marketing and sales* plans to achieve the revenues that you desire?

   c. How will you attract the *financing* you need to build and run your business?

   d. How will you attract the necessary *people* you require for business success?

   e. How will you *grow and expand* with new products, into new markets, when your business is successful?

5. Have you considered the following **strategic variables** as a part of your business plan:

   a. *Product policy.* Define the characteristics, design, and mix of products/services offered.

b. *Customer policy.* Define the specific types of customers you intend to sell your products and services to, and their characteristics.

c. *Promotion policy.* How will you market and sell your products and services to your customer?

d. *Distribution policy.* How will you distribute and deliver your products and services to your customers?

e. *Competitive emphasis.* In what areas are you going to develop superiority or excellence over your competitors?

f. *Pricing policy.* How are you going to determine the charge for your products and services?

g. *Financing policy.* Where and how are you going to obtain short-term and long-term capital?

h. *Investment policy.* How are you going to allocate the funds that you receive in terms of product development, research, sales, promotion, and your offices and facilities?

6. Does your **business plan** summarize all of the information that you have developed so far in this chapter. A business plan includes the following ingredients, in order:

a. *Executive summary,* which describes the mission of the company, the scope of the market, the demand for the product or service, and the expected sales and profitability of the company.

b. *Concept* or the reasoning behind your decision to

enter into the market to offer these products and services.

c. *Objectives,* which are your goals for the business in terms of sales, revenues, profitability, and growth over the next one to five years.

d. *Market analysis* and a complete description of your analysis, including the reasons you have to believe that there is a substantial profit opportunity in offering your products and services.

e. *Production* data, including a complete description of everything that you will need to produce and offer as products or services to the market.

f. *Marketing,* a complete description of how you intend to market, advertise, and sell your products and services in a competitive market.

g. *Organization and people,* a complete description of the talents, abilities, and skills you will need, and how you intend to attract and remunerate the key people necessary for the success of your business.

h. *Financial projections,* including complete budgets, break-even analysis, and expected sales and expenses for the next twelve to twenty-four months.

i. *Ownership* statement, including the names of owners of the company and a description of the investors required and the plans for raising the necessary funds.

7. Have you carefully **analyzed** every metric that you prepared for a business plan?

a. Be sure to thoroughly *check out* every important number for yourself. Are these the metrics that actually drive success with customers? Are these the measures that enable you to deliver that product or service profitably?

b. Check your *assumptions* carefully before including them in your business plan.

c. Remember, in a new business, everything costs *twice as much* and takes three times as long.

d. In good business planning, make it a policy *never* to trust anything to luck or wishful thinking.

e. Make it a habit to look for the *fatal flaw* in any business plan or important financial projection.

As the result of your answers to the previous seven questions, what **one action** are you going to take immediately?

_____

_____

_____

CHAPTER THREE

Surround Yourself with Great People

"The best thing about giving of ourselves is that what
we get is always better than what we give. The
reaction is better than the action."

—ORISON SWETT MARDEN

The greatest untapped natural resource and the most expensive in any organization is its people. Motivating people to make their full contribution to the organization is the fastest way that managers can multiply their personal effectiveness. It's the only way to grow a great company.

This means that the greatest improvement in performance and in results can come from unlocking and unleashing the latent potential of the *average* person in the business.

The People Equation

Getting the people equation right is the hardest thing you will ever do in business. When discussing this subject with Mark, Charles Schwab leaned forward as if to confide a secret. "Your job as a leader is to find, attract, and develop other leaders. If you do that, your business will grow," he whispered. "If you don't, it *won't*. It's that simple."

Chuck Schwab learned early in life to surround himself with people who not only shared his ambitions, but who were more gifted than he was in important parts of the business. If he wanted to make progress and get things done, he had to become a team leader.

Schwab discovered something entrepreneurs often realize when it's too late: He had great talent in one area and not nearly enough skill in many other facets of his company. The only way to sustain his success was by finding, recruiting, and empowering others who had talents that he didn't have. It is a skill that few entrepreneurs learn until they have a crisis that teaches it to them.

"Most entrepreneurs think that they're brilliant at everything," Schwab smiled wryly. "It's never true. I thought I was a bright fellow," he said (and he is!), but he admitted that he was "*humiliated* in subjects like literature and language." The second time he flunked they nearly threw him out of college.

"When your name is on the door you are responsible, more than ever. But if you actually end up doing everything, then the business is in danger," he said. If everything depends on you, the business can't grow. If it's all about you, you are just one traffic accident away from bankruptcy.

Until you can trust other people to carry the torch, your company can only get as big as *your workweek*. When you have found people you can groom to fill your shoes, "only then have you graduated from being an entrepreneur to a leader," Schwab said.

Their Company Is Their Mission

Schwab's company dodged the bullet that destroyed many banks and brokerage firms during the financial crisis because he already had a leadership team in place that shared his values. They didn't fall in love with sexy investment schemes that were short lived and dangerous. In fact, Schwab gained market share with customers during the "great recession" because the company's leadership team had stuck to its knitting. The company is one of the most profitable and fastest-growing financial services companies that consistently ranks among J. D. Power's leaders in quality service.

"You need people who buy your vision as much as you do. And because they love it, they also have the ambition to take what you did to the next level," Schwab insisted. "You want people with the energy to make things happen *for their sake* [not just yours]. They want to take your company on as *their own mission* and make it even better."

The best thing you can have going for you in business is to hire a team of people knowing that each and every one of them can be leaders in their own way. Benjamin Zander, conductor of the Boston Philharmonic Orchestra, says that you need people "with shining eyes"—those who gleam with enthusiasm, who can "lead from the eleventh chair." Great people do their job with pride from anywhere they happen to sit in the orchestra that particular day.

Why You Must Develop Bench Strength

As any venture capitalist will tell you, it's really tough to attract investors and get a decent value for your company if the only asset in the business is you. If a company is limited by your time, your ideas, your energy, and your health, then investors and customers are at risk. This was a real problem for Apple when news of Steve Jobs's health problems leaked out. The stock price swung with public opinion about his prognosis. It was not until his team could demonstrate growth in his absence that Apple proved to stockholders that the company's genius wasn't entirely dependent on one remarkable person.

As long as all key decisions on your team depend completely on you, the company can't increase its scale as much as it deserves. And a company that can't scale and grow won't last as long or make you as rich as one that does.

Great People Defined: Five Key Success Factors

Before you can attract and keep great people throughout your business, you need a clear idea of how you define a "great person." The critical measure of success in any business is the ability to get results, and therefore great employees are those who get the job done quickly and well, consistently and at high levels of quality.

1. **Great people are good team players.** Does your team work well together? Are they focused on doing whatever is necessary to make a meaningful contribution to team goals? You want and need people who treat each other with respect—despite what may make them different—because they share a common cause or goal. For that reason, they will help each other to perform well, giving support and guidance whenever necessary.

2. **Great people are more concerned with what's right rather than who's right.** When there is disagreement, it should

be focused on the issues—achieving the goal—rather than blaming or making excuses. Do you regularly create a "safe" environment for staff meetings, where people can address difficult issues without making them personal, or do people have to avoid tough subjects for fear of reprisal? If team members are truly hungry to achieve the goal—and are allowed to be frank and even argue about how to get there—they will be much more effective than teams that attack each other or whose members don't bring up important but challenging topics.

3. **Great people are intensely results oriented.** Your best players focus on contribution, on doing those things that make a real difference to your company. They set priorities and use their time well. They focus on key tasks.

4. **Great people accept high levels of responsibility for the outcomes required of them.** They don't require close supervision because they feel personally accountable for results.

5. **Great people consider the company a great place to work.** They see themselves as a family. They treat the company as if it belonged to them personally, and they treat their jobs as important responsibilities. Work life becomes a part of their "identity," and they socialize with their colleagues outside of work.

Building a Great Team

Ask any experienced executive or business owner about their biggest challenges and one item is always near the top of the list: selecting the right people. As a manager, you always have two choices. You can either do it yourself personally, or you can get someone else to do it. Your ability to choose the "someone else" is the true measure of your competence as a manager in the first place.

Peter Drucker said, "Fast people decisions are usually wrong people decisions." Perhaps the smartest thing you can do is to hire slowly and carefully in the first place. This dramatically increases your likelihood of making good choices and decreases your likelihood of making expensive mistakes. Hire as much for attitude, personality, and character as for job skills.

Your job as the hiring manager is to find people who will be effective in the specific context of the job they will be doing. If you do not believe the person will be able to do that, don't hire the person in the first place. Here are some critical tools that will help with this process.

The Art of Selection

The best executive recruiters engage in "behavioral interviewing." The first thing they look at in the hiring process is how people have behaved in their prior jobs. The best predictor of future behavior is past performance.

Don't ask people questions with "yes" or "no" answers. Ask them "how" and "why" questions. Invite them to describe a time when they had to handle a particularly difficult challenge. How did they work with difficult people? How did they solve problems and get results?

"I never hire someone who hasn't made a very big and memorable mistake. I want to hear what happened, what it meant to them, who it hurt, and what they did about it," said legendary banker Jamie Dimon, CEO of JPMorgan Chase. "If they're a high performer, they've swung for the fences; and when you do that, you're going to miss plenty of times. The key is to know how people behaved in the past. That will tell you how they'll do in the future."

The Law of Three: Test Drive Your Candidates

As Harvey Mackay said, "Hire slow, fire fast." Take your time in hiring. One of the best ways to do this is to use the "law of three."

Poor hiring decisions cost between three and five times the person's annual salary. Mistakes are not only expensive in terms of money that is paid and lost, but poor hiring decisions are expensive in terms of the time you invest, the time other people invest, the time that is lost that could have been invested with a better candidate, and even the cost of demoralization that occurs in a company with high levels of turnover. This is why top companies with low turnover insist on interviewing many different candidates eight, ten, and even fifteen times, often by multiple interviewers, before making a final decision.

There are several applications of the law of three:

■ **Always interview at least three people for a position.** Even if you like the first person and feel that individual is suitable, discipline yourself to interview at least two others. Many large companies will not hire a person until they have interviewed ten or fifteen candidates for the spot. The more people you interview, the better sense you will have for the talent that is available. The more people you interview, the greater the selection of choices you will have, and the more likely it is that you will make the right choice.

■ **Interview the candidate you like in three different places.** It is amazing how the personality of a person can change when you move the interview setting from your office to a coffee shop across the street. One of the reasons you want to interview people three different times in three different places is that candidates will usually be at their very best in the first interview. After that, if they were pretending, the veneer will quickly come off in subsequent meetings.

There is another important reason to change venues for each meeting. That's exactly what many employees need to be able to do to be successful in their jobs: They will have to work with many different types of people in many different locations.

■ **Have the candidate interviewed by at least three differ- ent people.** A practical method, one used in Brian's business, is to invite the candidate to go around the office and meet the different staff members. Afterward, all of the staff members get together and vote. If even one person disagrees with hiring the candidate, the person is not hired and the file is closed. Brian explains:

> When I was a young business owner and manager, I felt that I was smart enough to make all my hiring decisions by myself. I ended up spending half my time compensat- ing for having hired the wrong people in the first place. As soon as I began involving my staff in hiring decisions, the quality of the decisions went up to about 90 percent. And there was an additional bonus. When you have your staff interview a prospective team member, and they all agree that this person would make a good choice, they all lock arms and go to work to help this person become a valuable and productive member of the staff. By being involved in the hiring process, your staff has a vested interest in this person becoming successful.

The SWAN Formula

One of the best methods you can use in interviewing is called the SWAN formula, named after John Swan, an executive re- cruiter. These letters also stand for Smart, Works hard, Ambitious, and Nice. This may sound Pollyannaish or even politically incorrect to some managers, but it's a good, practical prescription for hiring. Here's what we mean:

1. **Successful people are smart, especially when it comes to the skills and competencies required for their specific job.** This is what Jim Collins meant in his business classic, *Good to Great,* when he wrote about "getting the right people in the right seats on the bus." People who have a gift for their particular job tend to work faster, make fewer mistakes, and are more productive.

And how do you tell if a person is "smart?" Simple. They ask a lot of questions. The questions should demonstrate a passion for your business and, depending on the job, the skills that are necessary to succeed in that role. The more questions a person asks about the company, the job, the future, the competition, and the opportunities for advancement, the more likely that person will be a valuable employee if she comes to work for you.

2. **People who actually want to "work hard" are more successful at their jobs.** The basic rule is that "people don't change." A person who is unaccustomed to hard work is not suddenly going to transform under your supervision.

"Chances are nowadays that you're going to be working far more than forty hours a week. Most leaders spend fifty, sixty, seventy hours a week—weekends and holidays—in today's competitive environment," said Marshall Goldsmith, one of the world's best executive coaches and *New York Times* best-selling author of *What Got You Here Won't Get You There.* "You had better love what you're doing when you're committing so much of your life in the office."

Great candidates are prepared to do whatever it takes to be

successful at the job. Unsuccessful candidates will immediately begin hedging and talking about how the job is a "good transition" between careers or how much time off they need.

Balance in life and work is a constant challenge for all successful people. But the only real predictor of future performance is past performance. Ask references to talk about how the candidate handled a crisis or a failure. When you check references, always ask, "How would you characterize this person on a scale of one to ten as a hard worker?" If the previous employer is unable or unwilling to answer this question, find another who will.

3. **Candidates should be "ambitious" and able to demonstrate to you why they want this particular job.** "Don't be a flame-chaser," warns Steve Miles, vice chairman of Heidrick & Struggles, a top leadership advisory firm that provides executive search and leadership consulting. "Find people who are anxious to be effective and ambitious about this assignment, not some future promotion or benefit. They have to live for today in that job, not chase the flame of future possibilities." You should ask, "Where do you see yourself in three to five years?" The more that the candidate looks upon the potential job as an opportunity to perform well and then move ahead, the better he will do the job from day one.

4. **"Nice."** When we say "nice," in this case, we mean people who are positive, cheerful, easy to get along with, and supportive of others. They fit within the culture of your organization. Their beliefs are in alignment with your values and the customers your organization serves.

To insiders, finding a *nice fit* for the job means you have found a person the team can trust and enjoys having around. Depending on the culture of the organization, that might mean someone who behaves with polite formality in a law office or who can snap a towel in the locker room.

When people-centric companies like Southwest Airlines famously insist that you must "hire for attitude," what they are saying is that they screen for people who share their culture and are in alignment with that specific job and the people with whom they must be effective in that role. And that's something that varies widely in successful companies around the world.

At Google, "We beat on each other hard during my interviews," CEO Eric Schmidt remarked about his early conversations with founders Larry Page and Sergey Brin. "We tested each other's intelligence, our ambitions, our beliefs, our integrity. They kicked my assumptions about everything! We took each other to the mat. And we respect each other more for having done that. Part of our culture is to continue to test each other's commitment to making Google great every day."

Alignment on Purpose

Warren Staley ran the world's largest private company, Cargill, like a nice gentleman. He is a sweet, down-to-earth fellow when you meet him. "But I'd never invite outsiders to my executive meetings," said the retired CEO. Those sessions were filled with table-pounding arguments among high-powered intellects and managers from all over the world. Staley would allow and even encourage the raised voices as long as the fight was over the issue at hand and they never resorted to name calling or personal attacks.

"If you were too quiet, you wouldn't seem as engaged or authentic as your teammates needed you to be," he observed. In his rough-and-tumble culture, *that* wasn't nice. "We treasured diversity in the real sense of the word—it's not how you look, it's who you *are*, what you know and believe—all from a unique point of view that enabled us to be smart and win as a company."

No Yes-Men

The point is that you need to find people who are in alignment with your organization's purpose, not necessarily people who look or sound like you. As Cargill's long-time CEO said, "What would be the point of adding overhead just to have a yes-man? Why pay to have one type of person who only agrees with me?"

Great teams are composed of diverse, impassioned people who may have only a few things in common: SWAN. They are smart and savvy, hardworking, ambitious, and nice in a constructive way that adds value for their coworkers and customers.

Cutting Your Losses

Building a great team is all about effective *hiring*. The flip side of the coin is *firing*. You must have the courage to get rid of negative or disruptive people. They can drag down the performance of the entire organization.

One of the biggest demotivators for your team is your unwillingness to deal quickly and courageously with people who should be fired. The rest of your team will not only respect you for doing that as a leader; they *need* you to do that as a leader for the sake of the team. Too often it is only in a crisis that leaders have the courage to do the right thing on behalf of everyone else who is impacted by a negative person.

Many times, the choice is made to try to "fix" the broken person, but it seldom works. The negative situation festers. The issue is not the right fix, but rather the right *fit* for the job. Letting the person go is really the best thing for everyone in almost every case.

Would You Hire That Person Again?

When you think about the members of your staff, continually ask yourself this question: "If I had not hired this person, knowing what I now know, would I hire him back again today?"

If your answer is "no," then it is usually too late to try to save the person. The sooner you let the person go, the better it would be for all concerned. The worst thing you can do is to keep people in a job where they have no real future. The kindest thing you can do is to let them go so that they can find a job that is more appropriate to their skills and personality.

Here is another question you can ask: "If this person came to me today and said she was thinking of leaving, would I try to get her to stay?" If your answer is "no," then you know what to do. As Jim Collins wrote in *Good to Great*: "Get the right people on the bus; get the wrong people off the bus; and then get the right people in the right seats on the bus."

Give More Frequent Reviews

The problem for most managers is that they don't provide frequent or frank enough reviews of performance so that they can promote or fire people when they should, without legal problems. Most managers and employees assiduously avoid honest reviews because they find them political and emotionally painful.

That's why it is so important to create clear expectations and metrics to measure what it means to do a great job. If you expect the performance to change quickly, then make the measurement daily, weekly, or monthly. Annual reviews, while necessary in most companies, are a disaster if there is no other coaching provided for everyone on your team.

Without frequent feedback, you unwittingly underappreciate the best performers and promote the worst ones. The more objective the measures you can create to demonstrate good or bad performance—and the more frequent or visible those measures are to the individual and the organization—the less often you will suffer the ironic embarrassment of holding back (or losing) great people and keeping the ones who don't perform. As a leader, you must tell people when the actions they've taken positively impact your organization's objectives, but also be equally clear to them when their behaviors did not create real progress. Do it quickly and objectively on the spot, without anger or judgment; and don't dwell on it. Marshall Goldsmith calls it "feed *forward*" when you advise people about what could be done better in the future. It takes some of the "sting" out of the critique if it's given quickly and focused on what to do about it now or next time.

Communicate Clear Expectations

In the last fifty years, researchers studying the methods of motivating employees and building great teams have found that the single most important motivator turns out to be "clear expectations." When employees are asked to describe the best jobs they ever had, they invariably say, "I always knew exactly what my boss expected."

When researchers looked for the foremost *demotivator* in the world of work, they found that it was the flip side of the biggest motivator. It was "unclear expectations," or employees "not knowing what was expected" of them.

People are inordinately influenced by the expectations of others, especially the expectations of others they respect. The higher up you are in an organization relative to another person, the more powerful your expectations will be in influencing the behavior of that person.

As the executive in charge, you must continually tell people that you believe in them and that you expect them to do well. Find stories of your own success and failure—and those of people you all admire—that demonstrate your empathy and support for your team. When you confidently expect people to succeed, to perform, to excel, to commit to getting the job done quickly and well, they almost invariably rise to the level of your expectations. They will often perform beyond their own expectations of themselves in order not to disappoint you.

The Environment Always Wins

Top managers are those who create an environment where peak performance takes place. They simultaneously put all the known motivators in place while removing the demotivators that inhibit performance. Decades of research into peak performance and motivation can be boiled down to one conclusion: Successful companies are those that create an environment where people feel terrific about themselves.

"Many leaders don't realize that the environment in which you work—the office, the work unit, the people and culture of your team, the incentives, and the attitude of your boss—all of these things directly impact your performance," said Jerry Porras, "Lane Professor" Emeritus of Organizational Behavior and Change at the Stanford University Graduate School of Business. Dr. Porras is also coauthor of the business classics *Built to Last* and *Success Built to Last*. The environment in which you work is a huge factor in determining whether you are successful. And the environment will outlast you, good or bad.

The Big Question: Are you providing a "winning" work environment for your team? If you asked someone whose business experience you trusted to parachute in to look at your business and listen in on what's happening at any moment (without you being on your best behavior), what would that person think? Is your workplace motivating people to perform at their best? Is the culture helping people or holding them back?

Great managers develop the ability to bring out the very best in their people by learning and "understanding what makes them tick, and giving them power to feel as though they are working as advocates on behalf of customers, employees, and shareholders," said Steve Miles of Heidrick & Struggles. "Without a great environment and clear support to feel they're making progress in serving customers, most people work at a fraction of their capacity," Miles said.

Your Relationship with Your Boss

The Gallup Organization has conducted research on tens of thousands of employees, and it found that perhaps the most profound issue driving employee engagement is their relationship with their boss. It impacts everything that you do as an employee; this relationship colors your feelings and affects your enthusiasm (or lack thereof) in your work.

The quality of the interaction between the employer and the employee is the key determinant of motivation and performance. Treat your staff members like partners, clients, essential parts of the enterprise, because they are.

People are inordinately influenced by the way that others treat them, especially their bosses and other important people in the organization. A look, a glance, a comment, or a compliment can cause a person to perform at higher levels all day long, and even longer. The quality of the relationship between the boss and the employee can be measured by how free the employee feels to express his thoughts, feelings, and concerns, and even voice disagreements to the boss, without fear of criticism or reprisal.

One way to achieve this feeling of well-being and happiness at work is to remove the fears of failure and rejection that inhibit maximum performance. As W. Edwards Deming said, "Drive out fear." The executive who can create a positive, high-energy, high self-esteem workplace will have high performance, low absenteeism, low turnover, higher productivity, and fewer mistakes.

Drive Out Fear

One of the best ways to drive out fear is to stop creating it as a manager. When you are consistent in expressing your expectations and measure them objectively, you build confidence and reduce fear in an organization. When you have more fun in the office and maintain a sense of humor—as long as it's at your expense and never your team's—you can significantly reduce stress in the office. Even those businesses where life and death are at stake have embraced joy as a core cultural fixture in their companies. At Southwest Airlines, founder Herb Kelleher's legendary affinity for humor was known to often energize his team and drive out fear because he was willing to be the butt of the joke.

"They pitied me, to tell you the truth; they realized how incompetent I was, and they said, 'We can't have Herb doing anything meaningful, but we like him,'" joked Kelleher when Mark spoke with him. "So what job are we going give him where he can't really screw up the company badly? So they made me chairman, president, and CEO, where you have no power to accomplish anything!" he laughed.

Kelleher's stand-up routine is funny, but it isn't a joke. He's making a real point about how he wants every flight attendant, every operations or administrative person, and every pilot to know they are more important to customers than the executives in the corner office.

Leadership is not an award or entitlement; it's a responsibility to the people who make your organization great for customers.

"Your people come first, even before customers," Kelleher said. Period. "Unless they're happy and motivated, you won't keep your customers coming back."

The healthiest thing you can do as a leader is to take your team more seriously than yourself. Driving out fear is a core value of companies like Southwest Airlines, but humor doesn't imply that Southwest is any less serious about safety, service, or success. It means that joy is central to the culture of service that makes this company tick. It's how the company enables people to show their creativity at work and humanize their interactions with customers.

The Three R's of Motivation

There are hundreds of books that talk about motivation, but ultimately no one can motivate you to do anything. At its core, all motivation comes from inside out—you feel an intrinsic incentive do something out of joy, fear, or other internal factors. To motivate the behaviors you want in yourself and others, there are three themes to remember.

1. **Recognition.** This is one of the most powerful motivating factors of all. When you recognize and celebrate achievements, large and small, people feel wonderful about themselves. They feel positive, happy, and valuable. They feel more competent and are eager to repeat the task or take on other tasks.

You can recognize people *privately* by telling them that they did a good job upon completion of a task. Even better, you can recognize them *publicly* by announcing to as many people as possible that they have done a great job. When you start a staff meeting by pointing out that someone on the team has successfully completed an important task, and you lead a round of applause for that person, you communicate to the entire team why this work is important. You dramatically increase your team's motivation to perform at higher levels in the future.

2. **Rewards.** Recognition is one thing and rewards are something else. People need rewards of all kinds to maintain their motivation or else they will start to feel that the recognition is just a "show" with no substance behind it.

There are two types of rewards: tangible and intangible. A tangible reward is physical or monetary. Sometimes it can be a bonus, a promotion, or just a prize such as a pen or a briefcase. A tangible reward is visible and drives home the importance and value of the person who has achieved the goal.

Some companies hand out a lapel pin with the number "100" on it to every salesperson who achieved 100 percent of quota or more. This small, tangible sign of accomplishment is something that salespeople strive to earn so they then have something they can show off and wear with pride for the next twelve months. Everyone in the company recognizes the reward and knows what the person did to achieve it. The lapel pin may be small, but it is a symbol of achievement that is significant to the recipient and to everyone around them.

Intangible rewards are also powerful motivators. You can take people out to lunch after they have accomplished an important task, or give them time off with pay. Give a few days advance notice so that everyone knows that the person is being taken out to lunch by the boss because the person did something important for the company. This is a powerful motivator. You can give people increased responsibility, or send them to advanced training to enable them to do the job even better in the future. In this case, you get a two-for-one benefit. Not only does the person being trained feel more valuable and important, but the company gets back someone who is even more capable of getting better results in the future. Everyone benefits.

3. **Reinforcement.** Another powerful motivational tool is "continuous reinforcement." This is when you continually comment on the employee's performance, both privately and publicly. If it is a big job with several steps, or a process that takes place over several months, you should regularly praise and reinforce your people at each step of the process or for each mini-accomplishment, even if they have not yet achieved the final result.

For example, a large complex sale may have several stages and take several months to complete, from first contact through to signed contract. The job of the sales manager is to recognize and reinforce the work that the salesperson has accomplished at each step along the way to the final sale. This keeps morale high and motivates the salesperson to persist in the face of the inevitable setbacks and adversity he will experience.

Find Out What Your People Value

The key to increasing anyone's intrinsic motivation is to align the rewards you give people with things they deeply value. This is not as obvious as it may seem, so do your research and ask people what they are passionate about. You may be surprised at the answers.

One of the dullest jobs anywhere is taking checks out of envelopes and scanning them by the thousands. Banks hire workers in vast centers to get this mind-numbing work done. Bank of America asked these employees what they cared about most. For many, it was going home.

But one clever manager decided that wasn't bad news. She could increase productivity and profitability by awarding a prize to those people who could get more work done in a day, with greater accuracy and speed. The reward was simple: When you increased quality *and* throughput—in other words, when you accomplished more than you did yesterday—you could depart early. She was delighted, surprised, and a little embarrassed to see productivity soar and the office empty out nearly an hour earlier.

Replace Your Employee of the Month Program

To build a great company, with great people, *performance* must be the basis for any recognition and rewards program, or it may backfire on you. At Schwab, managers were surprised to discover that Employee of the Month programs were often counterproductive. One problem was that some managers felt obligated to honor all the employees, which made the program worthless. Other managers honored their favorite employee, which lead to resentment by everyone else.

Both approaches miss the point and hurt your company. Employees will compete to achieve a goal, and when they do, that achievement itself should be recognized first, then the person who accomplished it. Leaders should be rewarding *behaviors and results.* Then the employee, who must be measurably associated with those outcomes, becomes a good example of what other employees can do, too. Jealousy is the result of focusing on personality instead of productivity.

That's why you should replace your Employee of the Month program with an *Achievement of the Month* prize. People hate the former and love the latter, as long as you make clear to everyone what level of performance it was that led to the recognition or reward.

The Four C's of Happiness

Zappos founder Tony Hsieh shared with Mark one of his favorite frameworks for people who are happy and motivated in life and work when you hire them. We like to think of them as the four C's of happiness:

1. **Control**—the feeling that you have freedom to choose your own outcomes; that you are the master of your destiny.
2. **Connectedness**—the satisfaction that you have many deep relationships that feed your need for connection to others.
3. **Cause**—the belief that you are part of something larger than yourself; something that will have impact and make a difference.
4. **Continual progress**—the certainty that you are moving ahead, achieving goals and milestones that make your time worth it.

Each person wants to feel like a "winner." How do you get the feeling of being a winner? Simple. By winning or making tangible progress toward winning! By getting things done. By starting and finishing clearly defined tasks. And by being acknowledged for your contribution.

Making Progress Is Key

People love to feel they are making progress. Psychologically, task completion is a source of energy, enthusiasm, and increased self-esteem. When people complete a task, of any size, they feel like winners—as if they have just crossed a finish line.

The more important the task that the person completes, the greater the increase of self-esteem. This is why the kindest and most generous thing you can do as a boss is to help your staff members feel like winners. You do that by setting clear priorities for their tasks and then by organizing the work so that people can complete those tasks in an excellent fashion. To help your people feel more like winners, give them clear goals to aim at. Be specific when you delegate or assign a task. Set measurable performance standards for what constitutes successful completion of the task. Remember, what gets measured gets done.

How to Focus on What Needs to Get Done

Write down an explanation of exactly how to do the job so that others can read it and do the job as well. Create a recipe or formula for success for each important task. This simple act will save you a huge amount of time and effort when you hire the next person, because that new person will be able to quickly learn how the last person actually did that job. Then your new employees can learn how to be winners faster.

Here are recommended steps for getting people to focus on what needs to get done:

1. **Set specific goals and deadlines for all assignments.** Make it clear what you want and when it needs to be completed. People can't hit a target that they can't see. When people know exactly what is expected, how it will be measured, and when it is due, you are setting them up to win. You are setting a finish line that the individual can strive for.

2. **Don't Pull the Plug.** "Competition doesn't kill companies—most firms get in their own way," says serial entrepreneur and venture capitalist Jack Jia. "We were running short of cash

and working 24/7 on our software product in a rundown building. Someone went into the kitchen to use the microwave. The fuse popped and the lights went out," he sighed. The computers went dead and much of their precious data was corrupted. Exhausted and frustrated, they lost focus and started fighting over meaningless details, draining scarce time and resources.

Just before they ran out of money, they called an all-hands meeting. "We laid all the problems on the table and invited each team member to contribute ideas and, most important, *recommit to their individual role* in our overall plan," he said. "Ultimately, one person must be accountable for each specific project outcome. That not only reduces the chaos, it also is more motivating for people to know they own—and can take credit and responsibility for—their own results."

Finally, a venture capitalist arrived to look at investing in their company. As the VC peered over an engineer's shoulder to watch a software demo, he reached down to the electric socket and pulled the plug! The VC didn't want to invest in software that was vulnerable to a crash. "Fortunately," said Jia, "when we turned the machine back on, the software worked perfectly. If the VC had done that two weeks earlier, we would have failed his test and run out of cash. Execution is all about each player's ownership of the plan!" Within three years, the company listed on Nasdaq and was worth over $7 billion.

3. **Create standard operating procedures.** The SOP should spell out the successful techniques, steps, and activities that made it possible for a job to be done well in the past. Standard operating procedures that document what has been done before, and what worked, make it easier for someone else to step in and do the job well in the future.

4. **Align skills with capabilities and interest.** Are you giving people jobs that they can perform successfully at their levels of experience? Are you enabling them to feel like winners? If you feel that you have assigned someone a job that is over his head,

take it back and reassign the person to something that he can accomplish more effectively.

Sometimes a person who is doing poorly in one job will turn out to be outstanding in another job. This is why you must move people around and give them opportunities to try new things. One of the marks of winning sports teams is that they continually rotate players from one position to another position. One of the rules at work is that "a weakness is merely a strength inappropriately applied."

Management by Objectives

Management by objectives (MBO) is a popular and powerful way to unlock the potential of your best people and motivate them to peak performance.

MBO is best used with competent staff members—people who have demonstrated a capability to get the job done in a timely fashion. One of the greatest desires for human beings is freedom. People love to feel that they are free to do what they want to do when they want to do it. When you use MBO, you give your best staff members the greatest possible latitude of freedom, automatically motivating them and inspiring them to perform at even higher levels.

The way that you use MBO is simple. First, you specify the desired outcome of the task, not the specific process to be followed. As a military officer would say, "Get to the top of that hill!" It would be the job of the soldier to find the very best way to get to the top of the hill, once the objective was clear.

Once you and the staff member are clear about the objective, and when you expect it to be accomplished, you leave the staff member free to determine the ideal method and approach. Only if a problem arises does the employee need to come to you for help or advice. This is often called management by *exception*. You can offer your own ideas about how employees should go about the task, but you let them decide based on their own knowledge and experience, and on the actual situation. Great people love the opportunity to "own" their work and have their work contribute to the mission of your company. When you enable them to create exciting new ways to do that, they will get things done faster, better, and more effectively than you could ever imagine.

The Three C's of Trust

All of the elements of management we've discussed here contribute to the most important factor in a great place to work: trust. People trust you when you make them feel valued and supported for their contribution.

Consideration

You can build trust with the three C's: *consideration, caring, and courtesy.* Consideration means that you continually remind yourself that people have rich personal lives aside from their jobs. You express consideration when you take an interest in your staff, in their thoughts and feelings, and in their families and friendships when they are not at work. The very fact that you demonstrate interest increases loyalty and commitment to doing the job well.

Do You Care About Me?

Caring is even more important. Whenever we feel someone cares about us, especially someone who is important to us, like our boss, we feel safer, more secure, and more valuable and important. You express caring by telling people how much you appreciate them and what they do.

Perhaps the very best quality for building great people is

Golden Rule Management. This is where you treat the other person exactly the way you would like to be treated if the situation was reversed.

Somerset Maugham once wrote that "everything we do is to gain the respect of the people we respect, or at least not to lose their respect." People are very sensitive to the respect of others, especially concerning the people above them, the people who control their positions and their paychecks. No matter how you might feel about a particular issue, always listen to others respectfully and attentively. Hear them out. Ask them about their opinions, even if you don't act on them. Treat them as though they are intelligent, creative, resourceful people and that their thinking is valuable and important. This causes people to feel competent and valuable parts of the business and team.

"Hire your people as if they were your boss!" That's what Jack Welch, legendary CEO of GE for two decades, demanded. He taught each GE manager to treat his subordinates as if he would one day be working under that subordinate. Because of rapid changes and promotions for performance within General Electric, this situation occurred quite often where a boss would find himself working for someone who had worked under him at an earlier time.

Treat Your Employees as Customers

Another way to show consideration and caring is to imagine your team members are important customers of your firm. If your staff members were customers who had the ability to buy (or not buy) large quantities of your product or service, how would you treat them differently?

Practice courtesy with every person. Thank people for their leadership and for handling difficult situations. Thank them for being on time for a meeting. You cannot say "thank you" too often, nor can you say "please" too many times. Just make sure that the compliments relate directly to constructive behavior rather than personality traits. Every time you thank someone is an opportunity to recognize and reinforce the behaviors and outcomes you want from them.

Between 65 percent and 85 percent of your costs of operation, less cost of goods sold, will be staff costs, people costs, personnel costs. Your job as a manager is to get the highest return on your company's investment in human resources. You achieve this by unlocking the potential of each individual: You hire carefully, assign people clear tasks, manage them positively, motivate them continually, and practice the three C's— consideration, caring, and courtesy—regularly.

When you do all of these things together, you will have a lot more fun and your company will become worth a lot more. The team will look forward to coming to work and hate to leave. They will tell each other, "This is a great place to work!" And, more important, they will actually mean it.

CHAPTER 3 CHECKLIST FOR SURROUNDING YOURSELF WITH GREAT PEOPLE

How people think and feel about doing their work is the key to triggering the reaction: "This is a great place to work!"

1. What are the **three most important qualities** and skills you look for when hiring a new person?

    a. _____

    b. _____

    c. _____

2. How are you providing a **"winning" working environ-ment** for your team and in your entire company?

    a. _____

    b. _____

    c. _____

3. What are **three steps you can take in hiring** to practice the "law of three?"

    a. _____

    b. _____

    c. _____

4. What are the **three R's of motivation** for your team, and how can you use each of them to improve the perform-ance of your staff?

    a. _____

    b. _____

    c. _____

5. If we conducted a 360-degree assessment of you—that is, we called your customers, your vendors, and key em-ployees on your staff to ask about your performance as a team leader—**what would they say?**

    a. _____

    b. _____

    c. _____

6. What are the **three C's that build trust** with your team, and how can you practice them more often in every employee interaction?

   a. _____

   b. _____

   c. _____

7. Is there anyone working for you who, knowing what you now know, **you would not hire again** today?

   a. _____

   b. _____

   c. _____

   What **one action** are you going to take immediately as the result of your answers to the previous seven questions?

   _____

   _____

Offer a Great Product or Service

"The man who comes up with a means for doing
or producing almost anything better, faster, or
more economically has his future and his fortune
at his fingertips."

—J. Paul Getty

A great product or service is the key to business success, and without it, nothing else works for very long. Fortunately, there is a simple measure that you can use to determine and predict your current and future levels of sales and profitability. It is this: Pay attention to how often your customers say, "This is a *great* product" or "This is a *great* service." Everyone in your company should be focused on triggering this response from your customers every single day.

Focus Single-Mindedly on One Measure

This customer response, every time someone consumes or uses your product or service, must be the focal point of all your business operations and activities. Triggering this response must be the vision, mission, purpose, and goal of all your business activities. Make it your business and personal reason for existing.

To trigger this response, you must set excellence as your minimum standard of quality both in the product or service you offer and in the way that you deliver it.

Philip Crosby, in his book *Quality Is Free,* defines quality as when "your product or service does what you say it will do when you sold it, and it continues to do it. The percentage of times that your product delivers on your promises is your quality rating."

What's Your Quality Rating?

Imagine that a market research company was going to do a survey and rate your company, your team, and your products and services against all of your competitors. The researchers would ask 1,000 customers in the marketplace how each company in your industry rated in their perception. If there are ten companies competing in your industry, where would you fall on a scale of one to ten in terms of quality perception?

Your quality rating is defined as the level of quality that customers and noncustomers give your product or service in comparison with other products or services that compete directly with you. You cannot improve unless you have a benchmark against which to make those improvements. As much as 90 percent of your success in business will be determined by how quickly and enthusiastically people say "This is a great product" or "This is a great service" after using your product or service.

"This Is a Great Product"

For two decades, there was one company that was admired for having achieved this response from its customers by almost every measure. Challenge yourself to see how quickly you can guess what company we are talking about.

The company was so admired that leaders in every industry would make pilgrimages to its factories on every continent to see how they performed their magic. "No one had a better culture of customer focus—they're maniacal about quality—and no one is catching them," said Best Buy cofounder and former CEO Brad Anderson after his tour of this company's headquarters years ago. Anderson was leading Best Buy's own transformation to become the world leader in consumer electronics retailing, and he was deeply impressed by what he saw from a company in an entirely different industry.

"Those folks won't be overtaken by competitors; they're too far ahead. To beat them, they will have to lose what they worked so hard to build," Anderson said.

His words were prophetic.

An Obsession for Quality

The secret to the company's success was an obsession for innovation and quality in everything it did. Managers were black belts in Six Sigma, lean manufacturing, and every new form of process management. There wasn't a quality method they didn't master.

Even the company's worst critics and competitors were forced to admit it was one of the greatest product and service companies of the twentieth century. It won accolades for being flexible, open minded, and customer-centric—perhaps the toughest things for a big company to be.

The most prestigious rating agencies gave the company top marks for innovation, quality, reliability, styling, and comfort. Although the products were originally created to serve the entry-level and middle market, quality and performance boosted their reputation to rankings commensurate with the best luxury brands.

Ironically, there was a time, decades ago, when products made in this country had been considered the bottom of the heap. But after years of humiliation, the Japanese business community launched the equivalent of a moon mission to become the best in the world. *Made in Japan* became a synonym for excellence and high quality.

In the remote case that you hadn't guessed it by now, we are talking about Toyota Motor Corp. But not just its *short-term* problems. We are talking about the importance of a company's reputation. And, in particular, about how your reputation for quality can literally make or break your career and your company.

Your Reputation Makes or Breaks You

Your quality reputation determines everything. The perceived quality of your product or service should be what keeps you up at night.

Much of Toyota's industry-changing ascendance in quality came during the tenure of the current president and CEO, Akio Toyoda, which makes the automaker's recent collapse of quality perception a temporary yet tragic phenomenon. He started with an ambition to "impress and delight customers," but then eventually lost his genius for listening to them.

You have to throw your whole heart into giving your customers the very best products possible, every single day. For every person who is halfhearted in the task of serving customers, there are at least 200 eager competitors waiting for just that chance to take those customers away from you.

Is everyone in your organization committed to serving your customers with the very best products and services in your market? Have you imbued them with an intense desire to be "best in class?"

Do You Want to Be Best in Class?

Akio Toyoda did. He's the great grandson of Toyota Motor founder Kiichiro Toyoda, who in the 1930s created an automotive spin-off from his father's company that manufactured automated looms for Japan's weaving industry. In one of its first great acts of customer-centricity, the company held a contest in 1936 for a new logo. Literally translated, "Toyoda" means "fertile rice paddies," not a particularly exciting name for a new car company. By changing the spelling to Toyota—which can be drawn in Japanese katakana in eight strokes (for good luck)—the company distanced itself from its old-world past.

After years of mediocre quality, Toyota became one of the best product quality stories in the world. The company learned to do everything right. It segmented its markets brilliantly, creating entirely different brands with radically fresh styling and marketing for each and every category, from the edgy and youthful Scion to the luxury performance of the Lexus. Only two car companies appear on the *BusinessWeek*/J. D. Powers list of Customer Service Champs in 2010: Lexus, which was No. 7 (behind Nordstrom), and Jaguar, which was No. 16 behind Charles Schwab. (The parent company of Lexus is, of course, Toyota.)

Toyota took huge risks with its Prius hybrid car, betting on innovation against enormous resistance in the automotive industry. Toyota has been so far ahead of competitors that other global automakers like Ford Motor today license Toyota's green technology to drive their "American-made" cars.

An Expensive Lesson

"I learned a lot," Akio Toyoda told reporters and U.S. senators at the heated Washington, DC, hearings called in 2010 to investigate Toyota's devastating quality problems. "We will really do what we can from now [on] to transform to the kind of company that will have people saying they can trust in our transparency and our customer focus."

He acknowledged that his company put growth ahead of safety—and failed to listen closely to consumer complaints as the company grew to No. 1 in market share. The U.S. government has attributed thirty-four deaths to alleged sudden acceleration in Toyota vehicles between 2000 and the spring of 2010 (the time of this writing), and Toyota has recalled about 6 million cars in the United States alone.

The slow response cost them dearly, and the Toyota brand may take years to recover. But here's the silver lining: Toyota's huge investment in quality for so many decades built an enormous bank of goodwill. In March 2010, in the midst of the recalls, Toyota sales jumped 42 percent. That's how important a reputation for quality is!

No One Escapes Poor Quality Products

Most automakers have suffered similar episodes in their history. Just a week after the U.S. Senate hearings on Toyota, Nissan Motor recalled 540,000 cars over faulty brake pedal issues that may also affect the fuel gauge. Soon after, Hyundai Motor of South Korea recalled 515 Tucson SUVs for a defect in safety devices related to air bags.

Then a week later, General Motors Co. recalled 1.3 million Chevrolet and Pontiac compact cars sold in the United States, Canada, and Mexico to fix power steering motors that can fail.

The terrible irony is that most companies are capable of better quality. They know how to build quality products or provide great service. At the very same time that GM lost its throne as No. 1 automaker in the world and fell into bankruptcy, the company still made a great car—the *Cadillac*! Too bad the rest of GM's products didn't meet that standard.

It wasn't long ago that premium automakers Mercedes, Jaguar, BMW, and Audi suffered a highly public disgrace for quality problems. These quality crises forced each of them to refocus on customers. And it worked. All of these companies have reinvented themselves to regain their status among the most admired brands. It's an expensive way to learn a lesson about how your customer defines quality.

What Price Means for a Great Product

The flip side of quality—in good or bad economic times—is usually price. Because price arises as an issue early in almost every sale of importance, many businesspeople feel that it is ultimately the determining factor. They believe therefore the price must always be massaged, reduced, spread out, or mitigated in some way.

But price is seldom the real reason for buying or not buying anything. If price was the critical factor, only the *lowest* priced items in any industry would have the greatest market share. Toyota would have never become the No. 1 automaker in the world. The automaker is a master of low-cost production, but never plans to charge the lowest prices.

The small percentage of goods that are sold solely on the basis of price are called *commodities*. A commodity is defined in this context as a product that is "undifferentiated." You'll see them listed in the newspaper in the commodities market: Steel ingots are steel ingots. Texas sweet low-sulfur crude oil is Texas sweet crude, period. The only way to distinguish among undifferentiated products containing identical ingredients and the same weight or volume is on the basis of price.

Your Product or Service Is *Not* a Commodity

The good news is that nothing you sell is a commodity. Everything you sell is different or special in some way. Your job is to identify your particular area of excellence, and if you don't have one, to develop one as fast as you can. If your product is available elsewhere, you can achieve a reputation for excellence by the way you sell and service it. You can find ways to make your customer feel special and better than any of your competitors do. You must refuse to allow your product to be reduced to a commodity, sold solely on the basis of price.

Take steel, for example. You would think that steel is steel, and usually it is, unless you find a clever solution that adds value for customers in ways that set you apart.

Solutions, Not Products

Stockholm-based SSAB has done exactly that. SSAB is one of the world's leading steel producers, and perhaps the most profitable, because it produces steel that is *not* a commodity.

There's always great value and margins in solving problems for customers rather than just selling them products. You might think it's a cliché that you must sell "solutions" not "products," but it's true only if your solutions actually add value. SSAB takes the risk to invest in R & D with its customers, forming customer/partner alliances to build prototypes of products using special types of high-strength, low-weight steel. One truck SSAB built can carry almost twice the payload and burn less gas. The result is that customers discover not all steel is created equal: Steel from SSAB can increase their productivity and save them money on energy costs at the same time.

Not surprisingly, when your product solves your customers' problems better than anything else offered by your competition, those customers are willing to pay more for it.

The No. 2 Competitor Is Always Hungrier

"We often find that it is the second- or third-tier player—who is anxious to become number one—who is the most willing to partner with us and innovate," said SSAB CEO Olof Faxander. "The number two or three player in any industry is almost always hungrier than the market leader.

"Let that be a lesson to those of you who might become complacent," he warned. SSAB's strategy has generated substantial growth in market share and higher revenues, despite tough and determined national and international competition. The company wasn't injured in the downturn like commodity companies and today has industry-leading profitability over competitors.

Differentiate or Die

How about leather? That's not a hot, high-tech, well-differentiated product category, is it? But one Mexican company became a very successful and profitable manufacturer when it changed the way it looked at the business and how it was serving its customers.

"We used to make commodity leather products," said Hector Cuadra, cofounder of Cuadra Boots in central Mexico. But when yet another financial crisis devaluated the peso once again, many companies were flushed down the drain along with the economy.

At the same time, new lower cost competitors in China and India emerged, and so Mexico lost its natural advantage in low-cost labor. The Cuadra brothers, Hector and Francisco, decided they no longer had a choice to remain a commodity business. They would have to change to survive or grow.

The problem was there was no way to beat Asia on price alone. "We realized that the only way to win was to add value to the leather goods in a new way, to differentiate it," Hector said. They already specialized in exotic leathers. But that wasn't enough.

Deliver Quality First, Then Price

In 1991, the Cuadra brothers started to compete on the basis of quality craftsmanship. They would model their business after the best boots that sold in the toniest European and American boutiques. They would create the highest fashion, most glamorous, handmade leather boots in the market.

In the process, they struggled to create a new mission, much like Japanese manufacturers did decades ago. They had to "change the image of quality you might think of when the label said *Hecho en Mexico*," he explained. They were obsessed with quality. They had to teach boot and shoe buyers about the quality they could deliver and "prove we had the best leather designers and craftsmen right here." It wasn't easy.

Quality Obsession

If they could deliver the quality, then they had a chance to beat European and other global competitors on price at the high end of the market.

It took several years of hard work, but the strategy eventually worked brilliantly and catapulted Cuadra to among the top leaders in the leather business worldwide. Hollywood celebrities now wear Cuadra boots to the Academy Awards. And Guanajuato, the historic community where the company is based, has become one of the largest and most fashionable shoemaking centers in the modern world.

The Four Little Secrets to Innovation

There were four essential lessons in product quality and innovation that the Cuadra brothers and others like them had to learn before mega-success was possible. We call these lessons *dirty little secrets,* because they aren't the politically correct advice you'll get in most MBA programs. They are downright counterintuitive.

1. **Don't follow the leader.** Cuadra Boots discovered through trial and error that fashion was too fickle and too ever-changing to allow them simply to undercut the price of the best Italian designers with a knockoff product. They had to have their own designs to give the product a unique character and appeal to the wealthiest customers.

"Sure, it's risky to design your own products," Hector said. "But it's riskier not to. You have to have your own personality. If you just copy the leader, then you're always giving control over to him for pricing, distribution, and marketing." You can follow the leader and he will take you right over a cliff! You have to break out with your own designs that work for your customers.

2. **Create exclusivity.** Lower end, everyday products—whether work shoes or stuff at the hardware or supermarket—need to be in stock and on the shelf or else you won't get the sale.

But some higher end products can benefit greatly from scarcity and lower volumes to keep margins high. Whether it's an exclusive watch, credit card, or first-class airline seat, people don't want to think it's available for everyone else. And customers will pay more for rare and exclusive products.

One of the world's most successful niche toy businesses is American Girl, which contributed $463 million in sales to its owner Mattel last year. The company strategically annoys customers by selectively taking specific $100 dolls off the market for a time to increase the doll's value. Brand-new "discontinued" dolls sell for $249 on Amazon and eBay.

The trick is to understand the subtleties of what quality and value mean to your customer. This definition is constantly changing, and you must change with it. This takes guts and a willingness to get it wrong before you get it right. The goal must be to align the product or service so that it is precisely suitable for that particular customer segment, no matter how lowbrow or snobby. It's got to match the tastes and tone of your customer.

3. **Keep in continuous customer contact.** Cuadra Boots opened retail stores to generate sales, but the brothers found it also let them keep a closer pulse on the whims of their clients. They could see which shoes sold and why, minute by minute. They could experience how their customers felt about which fashions worked or didn't. To keep costs lower, they needed to test designs as quickly as possible. While retail stores were a risky addition to their business, they provided revenues and an extraordinary learning lab. Fortunately, they have been quite profitable on their own.

Cuadra has become one of the fastest growing and most successful boot makers in the world. What is surprising, however, is how many design experiments are necessary for Cuadra to create the big winners in the global marketplace.

How many failures do you think it takes to find a winner? Would you say one out of four? Do half of all experiments fail? Well, it's much worse. And that leads us to dirty little secret number four . . .

4. **Testing takes you from good to great.** To succeed, Cuadra found that only 100 out of 1,000 products make the cut with customers in their stores. That's a brutal statistic for an innovative company. Their odds are one in ten. But that ratio of success to failure took Cuadra from good to the best in the world in its market niche.

Why Small Firms Beat Big Businesses

Would you be considered a professional player if you hit only a third of the hardballs you were pitched? In baseball, yes, you'd be in the major leagues. But not in the business world. Would *your* boss tolerate two failures out of three attempts to develop new products or services or new ways to sell them? Not usually.

How many companies do you know that would actually tolerate that many failures? Would you personally be willing to risk failure 90 percent of the time in order to finally create a huge success?

This is why small start-ups and entrepreneurs beat big companies every day. This is why most game-changing products or services come from outside the big companies. Face it, small firms should not have a chance against big, well-financed competition, but they win in business every day. The large firms have more money, people, resources, prestige, bigger brands, better distribution channels, greater market share of customers, and a reputation to go with it. But the large companies prefer to play it safe, to avoid career-damaging failure and financial write-offs. They *avoid* experimentation.

Everybody loves to talk about innovation. It's the sexiest topic in business, but it takes more courage than most people realize. Most firms don't tolerate or support failure and never will.

Are You Willing to Do Whatever It Takes?

During Jack Welch's tenure at GE, one of his teams created the long-life lightbulb. Initially, it was a flop in the marketplace, although today it's a big success. It was too early. Did Jack fire everyone? No, he had a party in which he handed out free gifts to the team and gave the highest performers plum new assignments. It was a noble failure.

The big question for you is: Are you willing to do whatever it takes to deliver a great product? Do you have the courage to support your team with many experiments, many of which will fail? How do you treat them when things don't work out as planned? Do you humiliate or honor them when they swing and miss? Do they get fired or promoted?

Risk Is Less Risky Than the Status Quo

When you're the underdog, you have no choice but to take risks. As an entrepreneur, you take risks when you have no other option than to swing for the fences in customer service. When failure is not an option, you have to take more risk, not less. The paradox is that you must fail more often—in fact, it's safer to experiment as much as possible because you are more likely to find the right answer for customers.

"Great companies take risks, but they don't just take *any* risks. The risks you take must be clearly on behalf of your customer. Your only job is to make your customer successful," said

Faxander of steel company SSAB. While price will always be important, even a steel producer can charge more than competitors and make a bigger profit margin if, and only if, the product helps the customer become outrageously successful or makes them feel great.

Four Product Factors Shaping Customer Expectations

There are four factors attached to any product or service that determine customer satisfaction:

1. **The generic or basic product.** This factor is defined simply as what you sell and what the customer gets when he buys it from you. For example, you go into an auto dealership and buy a car. You purchase a computer or new server for your business. You go to a store and purchase an article of clothing. These are straightforward and simple customer activities. They are clear and easy to describe.

2. **The expected product.** This is where the customer service equation starts to become tricky. The expected product is *unwritten.* It does not appear in brochures or sales materials. But failure to deliver on these unwritten customer expectations will cause dissatisfaction and, often, the loss of the customer completely.

There are decades of research on the role of *expectations* in determining attitudes and behaviors. Most negative emotions seem to be triggered as the result of frustrated expectations. The person expected something to happen, or to receive something, and was disappointed.

Everyone has had the experience of going to a restaurant and being seated and then waiting for fifteen minutes before a waiter comes to the table. It was never written down anywhere that a waiter would come to the table promptly after you were seated, but you definitely expected prompt and friendly service.

Imagine ordering dinner in an expensive restaurant. The waiter goes away and comes back with your dinner beautifully laid out on the plate. But then he drops the plates in front of you with a clunk and walks away without comment. How would you feel?

The point is this: Each customer has certain expectations, spoken and unspoken, conscious and unconscious, which you must be clear about and which you must meet in every customer interaction. People expect that someone will answer the phone within two or three rings. People expect that the company they are dealing with will be polite, friendly, and responsive.

People expect that a business establishment will be clean, orderly, and well laid out. People expect many things, both reasonable and unreasonable, and their level of satisfaction is largely determined by whether those expectations are met. You must be clear about what they are, and strive to meet them every time.

3. **The augmented product.** This third factor in customer service refers to the additional actions that you can take, or services that you can deliver, that go *beyond expectations.* They are extra. They are more than the customer thought she was paying for.

It is in the area of creating the augmented product or service that you achieve meaningful competitive advantage in customer service. This is one of the most important areas of innovation in building a successful business. You must be continually looking for little ways to improve the customer experience in ways that were unexpected.

Here is the rub. Once you augment a product and offer something that is beyond the expectations of the customer, it soon becomes a part of the *expected* product. Once the customer expects to receive the augmented aspect of your product or service, your failure to deliver it consistently and dependably will trigger a negative reaction on the part of your customer.

Not only that, if you come up with an innovative way of increasing customer satisfaction by augmenting your product or service, your competitors will quickly notice it and duplicate it themselves. It will only give you an advantage for a short period of time.

4. **The potential product.** The potential product or service is only limited by your *imagination*. It refers to anything that you can do to make the customer service more enjoyable. Your job is to continually think of ways, large and small, that you can satisfy your customer even more, and that will differentiate you from your competition, at least for a while. Again, this is a moving target. You can never let up or relax.

Make It Easy to Buy, Easy to Use, and Free of Risk

One of the most important attributes that makes a product or service great (and justifies the higher price) is trouble-free ownership. In our highly complex society, with so many products or services that can have problems, the assurance and guarantee of hassle-free ownership increases the perceived value of the product or service offering.

By making it easy to buy your product or service, by providing a guarantee, or by making it feel less costly with small down payments, low interest rates, delayed billing, and other options, you can charge more and sell more than your competitors with less desirable terms and conditions.

When we asked George Zimmer of the Men's Wearhouse where he thought of his famous slogan, "I guarantee it," he said it was Business 101. The most basic principle in delighting customers is to remove all risk from the sale.

Offering refunds to unhappy customers is as old as selling itself. Most high-end service companies have followed Nordstrom's lead with its unconditional money-back guarantees of satisfaction. Nordstrom sells expensive products to up-market consumers and seldom compromises or cuts prices. But it offers a sweeping guarantee of satisfaction. You can take back any product purchased from any Nordstrom store anywhere at any time, and get a full refund, no questions asked.

Ask for Customer Feedback

Fred Reichheld of Bain & Company, in his 2006 book *The Ultimate Question,* has made one of the most important breakthroughs in customer service and business success in the last few decades.

Based on years of work with thousands of customers and dozens of companies, Reichheld found that there is one measure that is more predictive of future business success than any other single measure. He calls it the ultimate question: "Would you recommend us to others?"

This is so simple and yet so powerful that it should be the organizing principle of all marketing, selling, and customer relationships. Ask your customers, on a regular basis, preferably after every interaction, this one question: "Based on your experience with us, on a scale of one to ten, would you recommend us to others?"

Then, whatever score you receive, if it is less than a ten, you immediately follow up by asking: "What would we have to do to earn a ten from you?"

Customers Will Tell You

The good news is that many customers will usually tell you exactly what they believe you need to know to get a higher grade. And if you do what your customers say, and then go back to your customers and report to them that you have made the changes they suggested, they will be both delighted and amazed. They will become customer advocates. They will tell other people about your conversation and how you reacted to their suggestion. They will create within other people a desire to have the same experience by dealing with your company and buying your products or services.

Reichheld's research shows how companies can develop what he calls an "NPS, a net promoter score." This score is calculated by deducting those customers that give you a rating from one to eight from those who give you a rating from nine to ten, and calculating the percentage of customers in each category. Most companies initially find they have a low NPS. They also find that, by continually asking customers how they can improve their scores, and then acting on those suggestions, their scores move higher and higher.

As a company's NPS increases, so do its sales, profitability, and repeat business. The most successful and profitable companies in every industry turn out to be exactly those companies that have the highest net promoter scores.

So, continually ask your recent customers for their feedback in terms of rating your product or service, and then implement their suggestions and report back to them. You'll get better and better business results, faster and faster, and soon begin triggering the words, "This is a great product!"

Feed-Forward Instead of Feedback

Most customers don't want to criticize you or disparage your product or service. They don't want to have a confrontation.

Here's a better way to frame the question: Ask your customer to tell you how you could improve your product or service "in the future" for the customer. When you do that, customers are liberated from getting into an argument with you and can instead focus on positive things that you can do to make them happier "next time." You can't change what happened in the past anyway. But you *can* change what you should do next time."

Many companies and businesspeople do not want to ask these questions. They are uncomfortable with the possible answers. As a result, they prefer to guess at their levels of customer satisfaction or dissatisfaction and are often wrong in their conclusions.

The very best companies, those businesses that start at the bottom and rise to the top of their markets, continually ask their customers for feed-forward, in every way possible. They phone them, visit them, bring them together in focus groups, have them fill out questionnaires and postcards, and continually seek input and ideas from their customers that they can use to make their products and services even better in the future.

It Is Never One Thing

What's missing from this equation is that customers, as a rule, don't consciously know everything you need to do to improve your product of service. One of the reasons is because there is seldom just one feature or benefit that instantly creates customer happiness. It is usually many things.

That's why it is important not just to do surveys, but actually create an ongoing conversation with your customers. For years, consumer research expert Howard Moskowitz would be asked by name-brand companies like Pepsi and Prego which flavor would be "best" or what "one thing" would excite customers. He was famous for predicting people's tastes on everything from toothpaste to presidential candidates.

Yet his customers would often be disappointed to hear Moskowitz insist, "There isn't just *one* thing that works for a customer. If you think of one universal solution, there isn't one. And there is no one 'best' product for everyone; there are only the best products for the right customer groups," he said.

Because they were hoping for one answer, his clients would be dumbfounded or upset by his remarks. But what Moskowitz was telling them changed the world of retailing forever. Three decades ago there was just one type of mustard or mouthwash on the shelf. Thanks to Moskowitz's research, there are now a dozen "most popular" flavors of each of your favorite brands from your favorite companies. There's not one flavor of Coke or Pepsi; there are dozens.

The Spaghetti Sauce Revelation

Author Malcolm Gladwell is a great admirer of Moskowitz. He often speaks about Moskowitz's epiphany on Prego spaghetti sauce.

After in-depth consumer tests, it turned out that consumers had at least three major taste preferences: *plain, spicy,* and *chunky.* Consumers could not tell you on a survey that they wanted one type of spaghetti sauce, nor could they come up with the word *chunky.* But they had these three preferences, and Moskowitz didn't learn that until he personally watched consumers make dozens of different home recipes in their kitchens.

"If you ask people to tell you what coffee they like, most will lie to you," Gladwell has mused. They'll say they want rich, dark full-flavored brew. Moskowitz knows that less than a quarter of the population likes it strong. The vast majority drink Starbucks sweet, weak, milky coffees, from mochas to mistos. People often don't tell the truth on a survey if they don't think it's cool or politically correct. But you won't know this until you watch people use your product.

Join Your Customer's R & D Department

The easiest way to figure out what products will sell best is to become an insider in your customer's R & D department. Whether you make sports cars, spaghetti sauce, or steel, resolve to develop the sort of "customer intimacy" that enables you to understand what your clients need and love at a deep level. What product or service will make your customer successful? That's the key to product quality and differentiation that will grow your profitability.

Ask customers what they would buy again and why, but then go out and see what actually works for them. Get in the kitchen and test as many new recipes as you can with your customer until you find the right answer. Dedicate yourself and every person in your organization to know your customers better than anyone else so that you are never a commodity business.

Customer Intimacy = Profitability

What do your customers really want and need? What can you do in every customer interaction to trigger the words you want to hear: "This is a great product" or "This is a great service" or "This is a great company."

Whatever it is, put your whole heart into doing it consistently, every single time, shoulder-to-shoulder with your customer. When you do, you will sell more, grow faster, and earn higher profits than ever before.

CHAPTER 4 CHECKLIST FOR OFFERING A GREAT PRODUCT OR SERVICE

1. What are the most important **values or benefits** that your most popular and profitable products or services provide to your customers?

   a. _____

   b. _____

   c. _____

2. What could you do immediately to improve your **quality ranking** in comparison with your competitors?

   a. _____

   b. _____

   c. _____

3. How do you make **innovation possible** in your company—including support for the people leading those experiments that fail?

   a. _____

   b. _____

   c. _____

4. In what three important ways do your products or services **enrich** and **improve** the lives or work of your customers?

   a. _____

   b. _____

   c. _____

5. If you had unlimited resources, what three things could you do to become the **top company** in your industry in the eyes of your customers?

   a. _____

   b. _____

   c. _____

6. What three things can your team do to become **insiders in your customer's R & D?**

   a. _____

   b. _____

   c. _____

7. What products or services should you **abandon or phase out** because you can never be the best in those areas?

   a. _____

   b. _____

   c. _____

   What **one action** are you going to take immediately as a result of your answers to the previous seven questions?

   _____

   _____

   _____

Design a Great Marketing Plan

"The power which resides in [man] is new in nature,
and none but he knows what that is which he can do,
nor does he know until he has tried."

—RALPH WALDO EMERSON

"The purpose of a business is to *create and keep* a customer," Peter Drucker famously said, "Therefore the basic management functions are innovation and marketing, because only they are capable of generating sales, revenue, and cash flow."

Marketing is the art and science of customer engagement. It's about determining what your current and future customers perceive that they really want, need, can use, and afford—and then helping them get it by creating and structuring your products and services in a way that delights customers and motivates them to embrace your mission as their own.

If you take the time to think through the answers to the questions in this chapter, you will sharpen your marketing skills, attract more customers, and make more sales.

The Big Question(s)

The following interrogative paragraph encompasses the key questions that you must consider and answer accurately, and explore again and again as market conditions change:

What exactly is going to be sold, and *to whom* is it going to be sold, and *by whom* is it going to be sold, and *how* is it going to be sold, and how is it going to be *paid for,* and *how* is the product or service to be *produced, delivered* to the customer, and *serviced* after the sale to ensure repeat business?

Most ideas for new product marketing *fail* because one of these questions was not adequately or accurately answered.

Four Key Strategic Issues for Your Marketing Plan

There are four key strategic questions that you must consider as frequently as possible, to test every product or service idea:

1. **Is there really a market?** Are there people who will actually buy your product or service? There may be a good reason why other companies aren't making this product available. To discover the answer, great companies try several variations of the product side by side and see which works best for customers. They test various price points and many different types of packaging and product names for the new item.

The only real test is a *market test.* Only live customers can tell you if you have a winner or not. Get a prototype, a model, or a written description or picture, and test the new product or service in the marketplace. Offer it, sell it, or give it away to customers and see how they respond.

Whatever you do, aim for immediate feedback. Don't be shy. Get responses from those you will expect to buy the product or service as soon as it is available. In most cases, your initial product or service idea is deficient in some way. But by changing it in response to customer comments or complaints, you may develop a product or a service that becomes a market leader.

Also, always assume that a competitor is rushing to bring a similar product or service to the market. Develop a bias for action. Avoid paralysis by analysis. Instill a sense of urgency at all times.

2. **Is the market big enough to make it worthwhile pursuing?** There may be a market, but is the market large enough to justify all the time, trouble, effort, and expense necessary to develop the product or service and bring it to market? Can you sell enough of your product or service to make it economically worthwhile? There are many products or services for which there is a definite market, but the market is too small to make it worth pursuing. Market research in this area can be invaluable in helping you to make the right decision.

3. **Is your market concentrated enough?** Assuming that there is demand for your product, and the demand is large enough, do the means of advertising and promoting the product exist that would enable you to sell to that market in a cost-effective way?

In his book *The Long Tail: Why the Future of Business Is Selling Less of More,* Chris Anderson argues that when the major competitors fight over selling the most popular books and movies, the profit margins for those few big "hits" get slammed.

Blockbuster movies and books tend to get deeply discounted in price by big retailers and flame out in popularity quickly. In contrast, specialized products have a "long tail"—they stay popular in smaller quantities and are sold at higher margins by more specialized retailers. Instead of going after the obvious blockbusters, Anderson advises savvy marketers can go after narrower, more specialized segments of customer groups all over the world.

Online services make accessibility to these unique customers easier and cheaper than ever. At the same time, however, the lower costs of entry also mean that more retailers are competing for the attention of consumers in every aspect of electronic commerce and making it harder to cash in on the long tail.

4. **Who is your competition for the same customer dollar?** We are always skeptical when entrepreneurs believe they have no competition. In meetings with venture capitalists, it is remarkable how many times you'll hear entrepreneurs say that their product or service idea is so unique and original that they have an unlimited market. It might be true that there is no competition for your product—because there is no real market!

Even if your product isn't out there (yet), there will always be competition for the customer's dollar. That's how you should think about it. Remember, the overwhelming majority of new product or service offerings fail because there is no market, or the market is not large enough, or the market is not concentrated enough to be reached in a cost-effective manner, or your competitor's offerings are superior to yours in some way.

We are not saying you should avoid inventing something entirely new. You just have to be sure consumers *think it's better.* That's when new markets are created and existing ones become vulnerable.

Five Attributes of Marketable Products and Services

1. **Your product is *easier* to use and more convenient than competitive products.** Many products and services do not sell because it is simply too difficult for people to buy them or to use them. People are busy and distracted. Convenience is important to them. Amazon has grown from the largest bookstore (both online and on-land) to one of the largest retailers in the world because it continues to be one of the easiest places to buy an incredible assortment of things that people want. Amazon invented one-click shopping—that is, the ability for consumers to buy many different products from one website with just one click. You can find products and buy them without worry 24/7, and get free shipping and guaranteed returns.

How can you make your products or services easier to use, hassle free, and more enjoyable than your competitor's products? One innovation in this area can give you an advantage over your competitors.

2. **Your product provides additional benefits and quality at the same (or comparable) price as your competitors.** These additional features or benefits can make your product more useful to the customer or easier to use. Your products may even be higher priced, but people are willing to pay for quality, or a special experience, if it reduces the amount of downtime associated with a lower quality product or service.

Charles Schwab rarely charges the lowest prices even among discount brokers, and instead emphasizes high-touch and high-tech service. Wal-Mart and Home Depot are not necessarily the absolute cheapest in your neighborhood, but they have built their reputations as a good value based on their relatively low prices, wide product selection and helpful service.

There has always been a cheaper place to buy a cup of java than Starbucks, Tully's, and Peet's coffeehouses. But they make the experience so much more enjoyable that customers eagerly pay more than they would elsewhere. In addition to coffee, the ambiance at places like Starbucks is conducive to hanging out and drinking more java, and bringing more friends and business associates particularly now that there is free wifi available to connect to online services. Even with countless coffee shops in the world, no one had successfully created a single brand that provided a predictable, consistent customer experience until Starbucks came along.

3. **Your service is *cheaper* than competitive products.** By using more efficient manufacturing methods, leveraging economies of scale, outsourcing to lower cost locations around the world, finding better distribution channels, or stripping down the product to its essentials, you can lower the price for a product that is clearly in demand.

The challenge you face with a strategy that is based on price alone is that often some tough competitor is willing to charge less than you do, particularly if that competitor is desperate for market share. At the end of the day, your product or service has to add more value to the customer even for low-price marketing to work over the long term.

4. **Your brand inspires deeper trust than your competitors.** Customers measure the quality of their experience with you against many metrics, but in particular they will compare what you provide with what image they have in their heads about your brand reputation. A brand is another way of defining your "reputation" with your customers. For this reason, it takes a long time to build a brand. It cannot be created with a couple of expensive Super Bowl ads, like the dot-com companies attempted to do in the 1990s. It takes many years for a business

(or an individual, for that matter) to develop a reputation, and it can quite quickly be tarnished.

Your brand is not something that can be allowed to develop accidentally. It must be developed by design, carefully and purposefully, in everything you do and in every customer interaction.

Define your brand clearly: What is your brand *today?* Explore your brand from several perspectives: What words do your customers use to describe your business to noncustomers? What words would it be helpful or useful for people to use when they talk about your company or your products/services? What could you do, every day, to ensure that when people think about you, the most positive words and images come instantly to mind? What are the promises that you make when you ask a customer to trust you and to buy your products and services? What are the promises that you keep after a customer has bought from you? Especially, do you treat your customers so well that they gladly and willingly recommend you to others?

5. **Your product appeals to your customers' desires** better *than existing products available.* That is, it appeals to the customer's need more effectively than anything else. Very few consumers would have thought to ask for, or could have even imagined, a world with mobile phones, e-mail, instant messaging, or Google before they were invented. But each of these new products tapped vast existing markets when they arrived. They scratch our itch for immediate gratification, easy access, and communication. They give us a greater sense of community with like-minded peers with whom we want to connect.

That's why online media, games, and mobile devices continue to steal huge shares of viewers from traditional television markets. We are inherently social creatures. We love entertainment that's interactive. Personal communication tools touch a nerve so deep they've become indispensable.

Why People Buy

People buy products and services to satisfy needs or desires, to *relieve* a "felt dissatisfaction." People buy products or services to *improve* their conditions in some way, to *achieve* a state of greater satisfaction or recognition than they would have enjoyed without the product or service.

■ **People buy benefits, not products.** What specific benefits do your products or services offer your customers?

■ **People buy *solutions* to their problems.** What problems do your products or services solve for your customers?

■ **People buy to save money or time, or to gain money, time, or recognition.** How does your product or service increase the amount of time, money, or influence for your customers?

■ **People buy the *feeling* they anticipate enjoying as a result of owning or using your product or service.** What emotions does your product or service satisfy for your customers? How will they feel when they use and enjoy your product or service? Does it give them a greater sense of status, safety, or well-being?

The basic motivations for purchasing anything are desire for gain or fear of loss. How does your product or service appeal to these needs? The more basic the need (e.g., food, water, security, health), the more simple and direct the marketing approach. When you are driving along the highway, you may see a sign that says HUNGRY? FOOD AHEAD. This is a simple appeal to a basic need. The more indirect the need (e.g., perfume, jewelry, cosmetics), the more subtle the marketing approach has to be. One of the most successful perfume ads was for Chanel No. 5. Catherine Deneuve smiled from the billboard and simply said, "Chanel No. 5. You're worth it." This simple appeal to a subtle emotional need made Chanel No. 5 one of the most popular perfumes in the world.

■ **People buy a sense of belonging.** They want to be a part of a community where they are recognized and can feel they can have impact. Perhaps the biggest breakthrough in marketing strategy in the early twenty-first century is the understanding that communities of customers can take a major role in contributing to your marketing plan (and product innovation) based on their ability to participate and share their knowledge and interest in your product or service with other customers.

User Generated Content

Think about it: The "content" that attracts viewers to Google's paid advertising is contributed by the billions of websites generated by the customer. Google serves up ads just in time as customers are searching to find what they want. Services like Facebook are taking this trend to a new level by vastly expanding the consumer's ability to socialize with other consumers. Users have created a half billion pages, and more than 200 million people log in *every day* to Facebook to send messages and create clubs with similar buying interests.

This online community of customers contributes content and, in effect, these users are actively marketing these social media services in the most powerful and "viral" way any consumer can: *through personal referrals.* They are signing up their colleagues and friends by the millions.

Marketing in the New Millennium

This trend is so powerful that many companies are outsourcing a substantial and increasing proportion of their marketing budget and innovation to communities of customers. Take Netflix, a mail-order and online video service that's cutting deeply into the market share of more traditional players in the video rental industry. Netflix has distributed 2.5 billion DVDs and video streams since its launch just ten years ago. CEO Reed Hastings created the Netflix Prize, a $1 million award to anyone who could improve Netflix's ability to make new movie recommendations to customers by 10 percent. Just as Amazon, the online bookstore, is famous for automatically recommending to you another similar book or another similar product every time you buy something, Netflix wants to increase its volume of business by doing a better job of predicting which movies that you would love to rent or buy based on your past selections. Giving customers great recommendations builds loyalty and boosts Netflix sales revenues.

The Nextflix Prize competition generated millions of dollars in publicity and attracted more than 50,000 participants who scrambled for nearly three years to find a solution. Making smart recommendations is core to Netflix's service to customers. By engaging customers in its research and development efforts, Netflix improved its product in a way that buyers loved. At the same time, the company turned thousands of buyers and potential customers into enthusiastic volunteers for its marketing and sales strategy.

How Are You Turning Customers into Evangelists?

How can you encourage your customers to participate and contribute more to your company's marketing and product development? How can you provide a place for your customers to talk with each other and share ideas and enthusiasm and challenges in your market?

Marketing is about understanding your customers with such

depth and clarity that you can empower and encourage them to be evangelists for your cause or company. When you walk into an Apple store, it is often hard to tell who's doing the sales and marketing and who are the biggest fans of the product: the customers or the staff? If they didn't wear Apple T-shirts, you wouldn't know. The company has hired evangelists—people who are crazy about Apple's products—to work in its retail stores.

Great marketing and great communities of interest turn passive onlookers into active customers and contributors to your product. One the world's "50 Most Innovative Companies" according to *Fast Company* magazine is PatientsLikeMe.com, an online community in which patients share experiences about thousands of medical treatments and procedures. It is a place to compare notes, recommend ideas, second-guess products, and get advice and share concerns about treatments with other patients. The community itself is a content and marketing machine that gets the word out to potential customers all over the world.

Unilever makes Dove soap, but it also engages in community building that helps the company market Dove brand products and add value for customers at the same time. Dove makes heroes of its buyers by featuring their ideas about health and skin care. Physicians, dermatologists, supermodels, and ordinary consumers volunteer to pitch their best beauty secrets in public forums that, in turn, influence other buyers.

Equally important, all this conversation with potential customers about potential products provides a living lab for testing Dove product and service ideas and creating entirely new lines of products. It helps the company better understand whether there actually is a market for specific products, and if so, which customers are the right fit for that product.

The Customer Is Always Right

The starting point of successful marketing is to remember that customers are always right, even when those customers may not be right for your business. Customers have a right to their opinion. They buy for their reasons, not yours. They vote with their wallet. Customers may appear demanding, ruthless, disloyal, and fickle, but they are always doing what they believe is in the interest of their goals and dreams.

They will change suppliers whenever they perceive that they can be better served elsewhere. Your ability to appeal to their real desires and to satisfy their wants and needs, as they perceive them, determines your success in business.

The Wrong Customers

Best Buy discovered to its horror that its massive advertising campaigns for ultra-low-priced products succeeded in attracting tens of thousands of customers. What's wrong with that? Millions of dollars and many years later, the company realized that, in some cases, too much of the added traffic in the stores was from customers who bought only those deeply discounted special items and not much else. Looking hard at the data, Best Buy found that some "teaser" sales lost money for the company, and some customers had a penchant for returning items (which created an expensive product restocking exercise).

"One of the oldest myths in business is that *every* customer is a valuable customer. Even in the age of high-tech data collection, many businesses don't realize that some of their customers are deeply unprofitable, and that simply doing business with them is costing them money," wrote Columbia University professor Larry Selden and *Fortune* magazine editor Geoffrey Colvin in *Angel Customers and Demon Customers*. Selden helped

Best Buy and other major firms scrub their client data to find that "it's typical that the top 20 percent of customers are generating almost all the profit while the bottom 20 percent are actually destroying value."

Why Do Customers Buy Somewhere Else?

Competitive analysis is the starting point of differentiating your product or service from all others.

■ Who or what is your competition? Put another way, who *else* do your prospective customers buy from rather than you?

■ What value do these customers perceive that causes them to buy from others and not from you? How can you neutralize this perceived advantage? How can you change your offerings in such a way that your potential customers prefer your offerings to those of others?

■ Why would or should your ideal prospects switch to your product or service? (If you cannot answer this question in twenty-five words or less, your marketing strategy is probably in serious trouble.)

■ What are your critical assumptions about your competition? Errant assumptions are at the root of most marketing failures. Could your assumptions about your competition be wrong? If they were wrong, what would you have to change or do differently?

Learn from Your Competitors

One of the best marketing strategies for you to follow is to admire and respect your successful competitors. What are your competitors doing right? Look up to them and try to learn from them. Remember, they have made an enormous number of mistakes and learned a lot to achieve their current position of market success.

One of the biggest mistakes a company can make is to criticize or denigrate its successful competitors. When a company does this, it blocks off all possibility of learning from its competitors and eventually learning how to outdo those competitors in some way. Instead, make a habit of looking up to your successful competitors and respecting what they have done to achieve success. In this way, you will begin to see opportunities to develop superiority to them in tough markets.

Sam Walton was famous for visiting his competitors and making notes and taking photographs of successful retailing ideas. In the early days of Wal-Mart, Walton would drive overnight and sleep in his pickup truck in the parking lot of a rival department store that was apparently doing good business. When the store opened, he would go in and walk the aisles, looking for ideas that he could then take back to Bentonville, Arkansas, and use in his own store. This willingness to learn from his successful competitors enabled him to spearhead the building of the most successful retail company in history.

Four Keys to Strategic Marketing

The application of four strategic principles to your business—specialization, differentiation, segmentation, and concentration—determines your success or failure.

Specialization

The company must clearly specialize in its product or service offering, providing a clear, specific benefit to a particular customer. In each case, the successful company stays within its area of specialization and strives to find more customers who want, need, and will pay for what it specializes in bringing to the market. The company can:

- Specialize in serving a *specific type of customer.* In the beginning, Wal-Mart defined its customer as "the person who lives from paycheck to paycheck." Everything Wal-Mart did was aimed at taking excellent care of that customer. By specializing in a particular type of customer, Wal-Mart became the most successful retail operation in the world.

- Specialize in servicing a *particular geographical market.* Convenience stores focus on a particular neighborhood, as do small stores with one location. Some companies focus on a single city or state; others focus on global or overseas markets.

- Specialize in providing a *particular product category.* Tiffany & Co. sells jewelry and luxury products that appeal to wealthy customers. McDonald's only sells foods that can be produced and sold at low prices to a mass market; it has created a system that specializes in offering value, cleanliness, convenience, a low price, and a taste that is consistent with customers' expectations every time.

- Specialize in providing a *particular service.* This is true for accounting firms, psychologists, massage therapists, and hairdressers. The company may specialize in a particular technology, such as computers and computer services, music and musical instruments, chemistry and chemical formulations.

"Build your niche. Ask yourself what you are interested in and then really work at creating that niche for yourself," advises business strategist Joe Scarlett, former Chairman, Tractor Supply Company, and founder of The Scarlett Leadership Institute at Belmont University. Ernst & Young honored Scarlett as the Southeast's Entrepreneur of the Year and Forbes selected Tractor Supply Company as one of the "Best Managed Companies in America."

"For example, Tractor Supply Company concentrated on the large-scale farming industry, but when I realized that 'hobby farming' was growing substantially in the market, I made it my mission to be TSC's go-to person for hobby farming. So pinpoint your niche and reap the rewards when you commit to building it," he insists.

Differentiation

The purpose of marketing is to communicate how your product or service is *different.* All of business strategy is ultimately marketing strategy, and all of marketing strategy is ultimately *differentiation,* the process of showing your prospective customer why your product or service is a better choice than anything else available.

Business success is determined by your competitive advantage. This is something that you do or offer that makes your product or service *superior* to your competition in one or more ways. Peter Drucker said that "if you don't have competitive advantage, you must develop it, or get out of the market." What is your competitive advantage?

- What is it that you do or offer that makes your product or service better than what is offered by any other business?

- What is it today? What will it be tomorrow in light of current market trends? What should it be if you want it to increase your sales and profitability? What could it be if you were to change your offerings in some way?

- Why does your ideal customer buy your product or service? What value does the customer seek? What does the customer want more than anything else from the purchase of your product or service?

- How is your ideal customer going to use your product or service to enhance the quality of his life or work?

To achieve lasting success in a competitive market, you need a "unique selling proposition." Your product or service must have at least one benefit that makes it clearly superior in terms of satisfying customer needs and that no other competitor offers. Put another way, every product, service, and company must have a clear and established area of excellence.

The identification and development of your *competitive advantage* and your *unique selling proposition* becomes the central focus of all your marketing and advertising methods. In every piece of promotion you emphasize and reemphasize the one thing you do or offer that no one else can offer.

Segmentation

Today, all marketing is segmentation. It is finding and focusing on just those specific customers who can and will buy from you the soonest and the most often and will pay the prices you charge.

Your job is to identify the exact type of customer who can most benefit from the superior features of your product or service. This person becomes your target market.

Here are some questions that you must ask and answer to accurately identify your most profitable market segment:

■ **Who exactly is your customer?** What is the customer's age? Education level? Income? What are the customer's tastes, attitudes, and interests? Each customer has demographic characteristics (i.e., those factors that you can visibly identify, like age and gender), as well as psychographic characteristics (i.e., the fears, hopes, dreams, desires, and attitudes that largely determine buying behavior). You must be clear about your customer in both of these areas.

One important psychographic quality that you must identify is the single most influential *fear* that would cause a qualified prospect to hold back from buying your product or service. Prospective customers almost always have a fear of some kind. Your ability to identify this fear and facilitate a solution in the course of your marketing can transform your marketing results in a very positive way.

■ **Where is your ideal customer?** Geographically, you can identify customers by zip code, residence, place of work, and/ or place of purchase. You also want to know your customers' place or position in their organization.

■ **What is your ideal customer's buying strategy?** How does the customer purchase your product or service? What is the sales process? Retail? Mail order? Online? Direct selling? Door-to-door? Newspaper? Telemarketing? Each customer has a buying strategy, which refers to the way that customer goes about making the purchase of a particular product or service, including the one you sell. For example, car purchasers visit an average of ten dealerships, narrow it down to three, and then buy from one. Women who shop for clothes usually visit three different stores before they make a final choice. Because people are creatures of habit, it is difficult to get them to buy using a different strategy than they are accustomed to.

■ What is the ideal marketing channel through which you can sell your product or service to the ideal customer? What marketing channel is your target market accustomed to using to purchase a product or service from others?

Concentration

Your company must focus time, attention, and money on selling more of its products and services to its very best potential customers. The 80/20 rule applies to customer concentration. A good rule of thumb is that 20 percent or less of your customers will account for 80 percent of your sales volume. Twenty percent of your customers will account for 80 percent of company profitability.

In concentrating, the company focuses its best people and resources on selling its best products and services to its best prospective customers. All advertising and promotion is focused and concentrated on those customers who can buy the most and contribute the greatest revenues to the company.

The Seven P's of the Marketing Mix

There are *seven* different areas of consideration that determine all marketing success. A change in any one of these seven areas can change your sales results dramatically.

1. **Product.** What is your product or service exactly, in terms of what it *does* to improve the life or work of your customer? The fact is that nobody cares what your product or service "is." They only care what it "does," or how it helps them do some-

thing. Define the ultimate result, benefit, or change in the life or work of your customer that your product or service will bring about.

2. **Price.** Is the price you are charging today reasonable, competitive, and profitable in today's market, based on today's market conditions? Pricing is a very sensitive issue. Small changes in your prices can lead to dramatic changes in your results. Sometimes, your prices are too high relative to your competition. You have no choice but to lower them if you want to stay in business. Many companies have found that by increasing their prices for their most desirable products by 10 percent, they lose a small number of their customers but gain tremendously in bottom-line profits.

You must also think of single pricing, volume pricing, discount pricing, variable pricing, up-selling, cross-selling, and down-selling. In a turbulent market, you must continually revisit your prices to make sure that they are properly calibrated to generate the maximum flow of sales and profitability.

3. **Promotion.** What are all the different ways that you advertise and sell your product in your market? Are there different ways that you could promote your product or service in different markets with different advertising media or different people?

There are more than twenty different ways to sell a product or a service. Most companies settle for one or two methods and pay little attention to the others. Sometimes you can dramatically increase your sales by offering your products or services through a different marketing or distribution channel.

Small changes in your advertising can lead to dramatic changes in the number of people who respond to it. The simple change of a headline or a tagline in an advertisement, in print or on the Internet, can increase response rates by two or three times. Never be satisfied with your advertising until you have more customers than you can service.

Your sales process is vitally important. Many companies have successful advertising that generates customer interest, but because their salespeople are not properly trained or managed, they are unable to convert those interested prospects into paying customers. Sometimes, a small change in your sales methodology can lead to dramatic changes in your sales.

4. **Place.** Where exactly do you sell your products and services? Are there other places where you could offer your products or services for sale?

Many companies go from direct selling to Internet sales to retail sales. Many companies in retail are offering complete online sales services. Companies are forming joint ventures and strategic alliances with companies whose customers are ideal for what they sell, then offering their joint venture partners access to their existing customers. Both business partners benefit from capitalizing on the credibility and established relationships of each other.

5. **Positioning.** This is one of the most important factors in marketing success. How are your business and your products/services thought about in the hearts and minds of your customers? What *words* do people use to describe your company and what you sell?

Imagine that you could wave a magic wand and choose the exact words that customers would think when your company is mentioned by name. What words would it be *helpful* for your existing customers to use to describe you to other prospective customers? What could you do, starting today, to leave the impression you desire in the minds of the customers that you most want to influence?

Remember, your *reputation*—the way you are known to

your customers—is the most valuable asset you have. You must decide how you want customers to think about you before and after they have done business with you, and then make sure that every customer interaction reinforces that word or message.

6. **Packaging.** How does your product or service look on the outside? Is there some way that you could change the way your product or service is packaged to make it appear more attractive and desirable to more of your ideal customers?

Customers are extremely *visual.* Unless the product has been tried before by the customer or is recommended by a trusted source, the only way the buyer can choose your product is based on its packaging. Does the name, the text, and the appearance match the customer's expectations or desires? By improving the visual aspect of your packaging, you can make your product look more valuable and desirable than your competitors' products.

In addition, the appearance of your physical facilities is essential in building credibility and buyer confidence. Make sure that every element that prospective customers see sends the message of quality and value, and builds trust and confidence.

7. **People.** This may be the single most important part of the marketing mix. Who is going to carry out each part of your marketing strategy? Do your people present the ideal image of your company and your products and services?

Customer-Focused Marketing

Everything counts. Every customer contact is either building or destroying future business. Every customer contact is either increasing your credibility or decreasing it. Every customer contact either helps or hurts. In today's incredibly competitive markets, you must treat every customer as though she was one of the most important people in the world. Every person who deals with customers must have this attitude. You want customers to walk away from your business feeling happy inside and saying, "That is a great company!"

Successful marketing places the customer at the center of all planning and decision making. It is essential that you stay close to your customers, whatever your position. Continual personal contact and market research are essential to ongoing customer satisfaction. How much time do you spend talking with your customers each day and each week?

Profit from Your Core Competencies

Marketing success comes when you profit from your core business. Start with your core competencies. These are the special skills that you and your company possess that enable you to produce excellent products and services and to survive and thrive in your marketplace. A major mistake that companies make is that they deviate from their core competencies and begin getting into areas where they do not excel. Remember, the market only pays excellent rewards for excellent products and services.

■ **What are your core products or services?** These are the products or services for which you are known. These are the products or services that you produce and deliver in a way that is *superior* to any of your competition. These are the foundation products or services of your business. It is absolutely essential that you are clear about these core products or services and that you continually improve in both producing and marketing them.

■ **What are your core markets?** What customers do you

tend to satisfy the most, and the most easily? Whatever your answers, you need to continually focus on these core markets because you are more likely to make more profit in these markets than anywhere else.

■ **What are your core advertising methods?** These are the advertising methods that get you the highest number of qualified leads per dollar of expenditure. This is where you need to focus your advertising dollars.

■ **What are your core selling methods?** These are the methods that bring you the most sales in the shortest period of time. It is essential that you continue to improve your core selling methods and processes.

■ **Who are your core people?** These are the most important people, both inside and outside of your business, for marketing and sales success. It is absolutely essential that you continue to appreciate and reward these people. They are the heart of your business.

Bundle of Resources

Look upon your company as a bundle of resources with the capacity to produce a variety of products and services and to sell them to a variety of customers in a variety of markets. You are not limited to your current product or service offerings. You can always develop or produce something else. Answer these questions:

1. How could you *sell more of your existing products* or services in your existing markets?

2. What *new products or services could you produce* with your existing resources, including your people and skill sets, equipment, and financial structure?

3. What *new markets could you find* or develop for your existing products or services?

4. What *additional products or services could you sell* via your existing distribution channels? Remember, distribution channels are often more important than products. Distribution channels exist and endure long after products and services have become obsolete and have left the market. Very often, it is a good strategy to design products and services that fit existing distribution channels rather than the other way around.

5. What *additional distribution channels could you develop* for your existing products or services?

6. Finally, what *new products or services could you sell* through new distribution channels?

Answering any one of these questions precisely and creatively can change the entire direction of your business.

Focus on Customer Creation

The purpose of marketing is to make selling *unnecessary*. Although this seldom happens, the aim of the entire marketing effort is to present such an overwhelming case to your customers that they simply buy as the result of your marketing and promotional efforts. The more dynamic and creative the marketing function in a company, the more sales you can expect and the higher the level of profitability in the organization.

A great marketing plan is one that attracts a steady stream of qualified prospects who want, need, can afford, and will pay for what you sell now or in the future. "No matter how small or large your company, don't compromise on going through the effort to create your marketing plan and think it through carefully, even if it's just a few pages," says business adviser Julie Woods-Moss, former President of British Telecom's Strategy & Marketing. "If you can't be clear about your value proposition, no one else can!"

In short, a good marketing plan works. It presents the right appeal to the right prospective customers in the right way to cause them to respond. Your advertising triggers the reaction "That's for me!" as soon as a prospective customer sees your product or reads your marketing message.

Good Advertising

Good advertising causes a prospective customer to say, "I want that!"

Herbalife, a multibillion-dollar diet and nutrition company, has its distributors wear a round button with a blinking red light that captures attention. On the button are the words LOSE WEIGHT NOW. ASK ME HOW.

For a qualified prospect, one who is overweight and concerned about that condition, this is the perfect advertising message. It simultaneously triggers the responses "That's for me!" and "I want that!"

Good advertising emphasizes the unique selling proposition of the product or service that you offer. It attracts prospects and customers at a low cost of acquisition. It illustrates the clear competitive advantage that your product or service has in comparison with those offered by competing businesses.

If your advertising is good, it should be clear to a ten-year-old why a qualified prospect would want to buy and use your product or service. It cannot be fuzzy or unclear. It must cut straight to the heart of the most pressing need that a prospect

Is Your Phone Ringing?

Good marketing arouses both desire and curiosity. The value offering in the advertising triggers the response: "How do you do that?"

Effective advertising works. Period. It triggers an immediate response from qualified prospects. It causes prospects to voluntarily reach out mentally and emotionally for what you are offering.

Some years ago, we were advertising a service on the radio. But our response level was low and disappointing. One day, the head of an advertising agency called us up and asked how our campaign was doing. We bluffed a little bit and avoided answering his question. He then said, "I have just one question for you: Is your phone ringing?"

As it happened, our phone was not ringing even though our phone number was repeated several times during each radio spot. He took a closer look at what customers needed and wanted. He reviewed what fears and desires drove their behavior. He offered to rewrite our advertising and get our phone ringing. We accepted his offer and he delivered. By the next week, our phone was ringing off the hook and our promotion was successful. Ever since then, whenever we think of good marketing and advertising at Brian Tracy International, we ask that fundamental question.

The simplest way to measure the effectiveness of an advertising campaign is whether it causes your phone to ring and your cash register to jingle. It triggers immediate responses from qualified buyers.

would have that would cause him to reach out for what you are selling.

Measure Your Results

The only way to determine whether a particular advertising approach is working is to try it out, again and again. The three most important words in advertising are "test, test, test."

In advertising, you can change one variable at a time and compare the results with your previous version. Sometimes, you can change more than one variable. Whether it's Procter & Gamble or BestBuy.com, marketers are constantly testing A and B versions of the same promotions to see what works best in attracting prospective customers. Ultimately, the only question that matters is, *Does it work?*

Customers have more important things to do than pay attention to your advertising. When they do, they are disengaged, suspicious, skeptical, cautious, and careful. To get them to buy from you the first time is both an art and a science. The benefit you offer must be so attractive that people are willing to give it a try. Then you must make it a "no-brainer," a low-risk, no-risk proposal. Offer a free trial and a money-back guarantee. These techniques are as old as business itself—because they work.

The way you can tell what's working is by measuring lead generation costs. One of the most important numbers in any business is the cost of customer acquisition, and lead generation is a major component of that cost. The only way that you can accurately measure the effectiveness of your marketing efforts is the number of qualified leads generated each time your advertising appears in the media. You then measure and compare the cost paid for each lead generated.

Risk-Reversal Marketing

To sell more of your product or service, you need to understand your potential customer's biggest fear about doing business with you, and then shift that risk to yourself. This is called risk-reversal marketing. The key to the success of this method is that your additional bottom-line income will be greater than the increased liability.

Risk-reversal marketing turned a little company called Shoes for Crews into a $100 million industry player. The company makes work boots that are often standard-issue uniform items for many jobs. The good news is that employers can deduct the cost of the work shoes directly from workers' paychecks. The bad news is that employees can also buy those boots anywhere else. How could entrepreneur Matthew Smith find a way to make customers care about his high-quality shoes in a commodity market for work boots?

Smith had an epiphany. Employers worried about workers compensation claims when employees were hurt on the job. So Smith guaranteed that workers would not slip in his shoes—and he'd pay the claim if they did. He offered a $500 warranty on a $50 product! Then he gradually increased the warranty to $5,000. It was a smashing success. More than 90 percent of the biggest restaurant chains recommend the Shoes for Crews brand for their workers.

What about claims? Shoes for Crews pays hundreds of claims every year, but it adds up to less than one or two percent of sales.

Customers are downright shocked at the outrageous offer, and Smith wins lifelong customers. Combining this sweeping guarantee with quality products and excellent customer service continually causes people to say, "This is a great place to shop."

See Yourself as a Partner

Marketing and advertising ultimately are about credibility and accountability. Think of yourself as your customer's business partner. You are already investing time and resources in your customer every day. Now take it a step further. Imagine that you have put money directly into your customer's business, as if you were a venture capitalist. How would you behave then? You would want the customer to be successful at a whole new level. You would want them to grow and prosper for the long term.

Jordan Zimmerman, founder of an ad agency that bears his name, has billings of over $2.6 billion. He calls every client *every single day* and monitors their business as if he were an owner.

The executives who manage each customer account plan their day around their client's sales data from the day before. "We study the data from every store every single business day," he said. When you call your customer every day, you can't help but be held accountable for their success and challenges. "If something works, we know it. If it isn't, we can try something new instantly. We act quickly and work to grow the business 24/7." Zimmerman Advertising behaves like a member of the client's operating management and, as a result, most of the brands he represents have prospered even in difficult market environments.

"I love advertising and marketing, but more important, I'm a partner looking out for my customer's success every day," Zimmerman said. In business, that's when you become indispensable.

Do the same in your own business. Carefully monitor and control your marketing efforts and always be willing to change them if you and your customers are not getting the best results. Your job is to make your customers more successful and to exceed their expectations every business day.

CHAPTER 5 CHECKLIST TO DEVELOP A GREAT MARKETING PLAN

What exactly are you selling, and *to whom* is it going to be sold, and *by whom* is it going to be sold, and *how* is it going to be sold, and *how* is it going to be paid for, and *how* is the product or service to be produced and delivered to the customer, and *how* is it to be serviced after the sale?

This "big question" is really a series of strategic issues that capture every key point in the development of your marketing plan. A change in your answer to any one question can change the effectiveness of your marketing and the profitability of your business.

1. **What exactly do you sell**, defined in terms of what your product or service actually does to improve the life or work of your customer?

   a. _____

   b. _____

   c. _____

2. What is your competitive advantage? What are the **core competencies** that make your product or service superior to anything else available?

   a. _____

   b. _____

   c. _____

3. **Describe your ideal customer.** Who wants, needs, and is most willing to pay for the benefits provided by your product or service?

   a. _____

   b. _____

   c. _____

4. What are your **most effective marketing methods**? How do you attract the greatest number of qualified customers?

   a. _____

   b. _____

   c. _____

5. Who or what are your biggest competitors in the sale of your products or services, and **how do you differentiate** your products or services from those of your competitors?

   a. _____

   b. _____

   c. _____

6. How can you encourage your customers to participate and contribute more to your company's marketing and product development? **How can you create a community for your customers** to share ideas, enthusiasm, and challenges in your market?

a. _____

b. _____

c. _____

7. **What changes could you make** in your products, prices, promotions, places, positioning, packaging, or people—the seven P's of your marketing mix—to make your offerings more desirable to your target market?

a. _____

b. _____

c. _____

What **one action** are you going to take immediately as the result of your answers to the previous seven questions?

_____

_____

_____

CHAPTER SIX

Perfect a Great Sales Process

"Nothing happens until a sale takes place."

—RED MOTLEY

M any businesses are started by people with no sales experience. They may be entrepreneurs who love a product, or invented one, and now they have to sell it.

But they have no idea what goes on in the interaction between the careful, cautious, skeptical potential customer and the salesperson. They think that sales fall from the sky, like the rain, if you have a good enough product or service. They are then astonished when their companies run out of customers, cash, and credit, and they go bankrupt. The adage, "If you build it, they will come," is rarely true. In business, "they"—the customers—will come only if they want to.

In today's environment, any business that wants to success-fully sell its products and services must begin by understanding exactly who its customers are and why they buy.

The New Realities of Selling

There is more competition for the business than ever before, and the competition is getting stiffer every week and every month.

Customers today are tougher to sell to than ever before. They are more demanding with regard to quality, service, and value. Customers today have more choices and therefore less urgency to decide. Customers are impatient; they want every-thing now.

What Customers Want

In selling a great product or service, perhaps the most impor-tant word is *consistency.* Your customer must consistently enjoy the results that you promised to induce the customer to buy your product in the first place. If your product delivers on its promises 90 percent of the time, then your quality rating is 90 percent. Your ultimate goal is to achieve a rating of 100 percent, which is the rating that you earn when your product or service consistently and dependably delivers on your promises 100 per-cent of the time. This is what causes customers to say you have a "great product!"

Three Types of Customers

There are three types of customers to whom you might be sell-ing. First, there are businesses that use your product or service in the course of their activities. Second, there are businesses that resell your product or service in the market. Third, there are consumers who buy and use your product or service to enhance their personal lives. Each of these customers has a different set of needs to which you must appeal.

All buying behavior, however, is aimed at the achievement of a definite *improvement* of some kind. The product or service must solve a problem, satisfy a need, or achieve a goal. To offer a great product or service, you must be absolutely clear about what your product or service is intended to accomplish for your customer.

The goal of any business is to serve its customers and generate a profit, to generate revenues in excess of costs. A business can accomplish profitability by selling more of its products and services, by selling them at a higher price, by achieving repeat business, or by lowering the costs involved in selling, producing, and delivering the product or service in the first place.

Selling Great Products to Business Customers

Decision makers responsible for business purchases think continually about the bottom line, about how your product or service will affect *net profits*. In the simplest terms, in selling to a business, your primary aim must be to demonstrate that your product or service will generate greater efficiency, effectiveness, and therefore more bottom-line income or savings than the amount the customer will pay for what you sell.

Ideally, in selling to businesses, your job is to convince the decision maker that your product is, whenever possible, actually "free, plus a profit." In other words, your product contributes to your customer's bottom line; it makes your customers more profitable and successful than they would have been without it.

Your job is to demonstrate that, if the business purchases your product or service, the benefit that it can expect in net dollar terms will be well in excess of the cost. If your product costs $100,000 and saves or makes the business customer $50,000 per year, and continues to perform effectively for five years, the customer will get a 50 percent return on his money each year for two years, and then a net of $50,000 to the bottom line for the next three years. In this case, your product or service is "free, plus a profit."

Of course, there are many products and services that businesses buy to satisfy ego or aesthetic desires. But even a product or service designed to improve the attractiveness or beauty of a business office or a location is ultimately aimed at attracting and keeping more customers and making more profitable sales.

Business customers want answers to four questions before committing to buying a product or service:

1. What is the value equation? (relative cost, quality, reliability)

2. How much do I get back? (return on investment, assets, clients)

3. How soon do I get it back, or on what schedule? (time to payback)

4. How sure can I be that I will actually enjoy the bottom-line financial benefits that you are offering? (risk management and guarantee issues)

These questions are usually *unspoken,* but they exist in the mind of the buyer. If you fail to answer them satisfactorily in the course of your sales presentation, the customer will put off the buying decision, or not buy at all.

The single most important determinant of whether a business buys your product or service and considers it to be a high-quality offering is *time to payback*. The sooner your product or service pays for itself and begins yielding a net financial benefit to your customer, the faster and easier it is for the customer to purchase your product or service. Your ability to demonstrate rapid payback and to convince the customer that he will enjoy this result with a high degree of certainty is central to your making the sale in the first place.

Selling Great Products to Wholesalers or Retailers

The motivation of this second type of customer is very different from the business customer. The primary concern of the retailer is net profit as the result of either high turnover or high profitability per unit sold, or both.

Of course, retailers want their customers to be happy. For this reason, they will be demanding high quality in the product you offer and requiring that you guarantee absolute satisfaction to their customers.

At one time, you had to offer an excellent product or service—one that delivered on your promises consistently—in order to increase sales, market share, and profitability. But today, your product or service must be excellent for you to even enter into a competitive market. Wholesalers and retailers have a lot of choices when it comes to products they will carry and services they will offer.

Selling Great Products to Consumers

The third type of customer that you sell to will be the consumer. The consumer or end user of your product or service has different motivations from the business customer or other resellers.

Consumers seek improvement in their life or work. The consumer is more concerned about what your product or service "does" rather than what it "is."

Customers are emotional. Their primary motivation to purchase what you sell is their anticipation of how they will *feel* after having bought from you. Will they feel happy? Proud? Secure? More attractive? More respected? Richer? More confident?

There is a difference between consumer needs and wants. They are not the same. People may *need* to be healthy, thin, and fit, but they *want* to eat delicious foods in large quantities. A product or service that seems like a logical choice may not be an emotional preference. Your ability to separate these issues is essential for your success in triggering the desired consumer response.

What do consumers really want? When grocers such as Whole Foods Market promoted the personal health benefits and enhanced environmental impact of organic foods, it wasn't enough. For consumers to pay more, the food had to taste much better, too. When consumers discovered that organic ingredients made fancy cuisine taste great, a multibillion-dollar industry sprang out of the commodity grocery business.

When you go to a restaurant and order a meal, you want to be able to say afterward that "This is a great restaurant." The goal of the restaurateur and every person who interacts with the dining customer must be aimed at triggering this response.

To offer any great product or service, you must be absolutely clear about the feeling that your product or service will create for your potential customer. It is only when you can generate that feeling and deliver on your promise that customers will call it a "great" product.

Three Ways to Increase Sales

There are basically three ways to increase sales:

1. **Increase the number of transactions.** Volume can be accomplished through marketing and advertising, using special promotions, discounts, and a variety of other means to get customers to buy from you for the first time.

2. **Expand the size of each transaction.** Once you have attracted a prospect, you can up-sell, cross-sell, and even down-sell if the customer cannot afford the main product or service.

3. **Increase the frequency of purchases.** You can take such good care of the customer that she buys again and again. This is obviously the most efficient type of customer interaction—selling more to existing buyers. All good business is about "exceeding customer expectations." The key measure of customer satisfaction is repeat business. It is not possible for a business to succeed in the long term unless it takes such good care of its customers that they return again and again. This is only possible when the business can trigger the response, "This is a great product!"

Set Your Own Bar

Your competitors wake up every morning thinking about how to get your customers, take your business away from you, and put you out of business, if possible. Your competitors are often obsessed with winning your customers' attention. Just like you, they realize that there is fierce competition for customer dollars, and they are determined to get as many of them as possible, even if that means that you get none at all. The best salespeople are obsessive about follow-up and the relentless pursuit of the best prospects.

Your job is to learn everything you possibly can about your competitors so that you can assess their strengths and weaknesses in the marketplace, then set your own bar. With more and more salespeople descending on fewer and fewer customers, persistence and knowledge matter more than ever before.

In *Blue Ocean Strategy: How to Create Uncontested Market Space and Make Competition Irrelevant,* W. Chan Kim and Renee Mauborgne encourage you to set your own buying criteria for your business rather than rely on your competitors to determine quality, price, and ultimately, the survival of your products and services. They argue that you can sidestep "red oceans" of competition by not following their lead, by redefining a market and setting your own new rules.

Their favorite example is Cirque du Soleil, a company that created an entirely new way for people to think about the circus and, in turn, resuscitated a dying industry. It was a brilliant and fresh way to recapture entertainment dollars and it caught competitors flat-footed. Cirque du Soleil redefined the rules and reinvented the customer experience, and its new style of entertainment product sold itself.

The Measure of Sales Success

Customer retention is the key to sales success. Single-purchase customers are too hard and expensive to acquire. Your focus must be on the second sale, and the third sale. Your goal must be resales to the same customer, over and over. In addition, your goal should be to get referrals from your satisfied customers.

The most important sale is not the first sale; it is the *second.*

You can win the first sale with promises, special offers, and discounts, but you only attract repeat business when your customers feel that you delivered on your promises. This causes them to prefer to buy from you again rather than someone else.

The second sale takes approximately one-tenth of the time and expense to attract, and it is therefore much easier and more profitable than the first sale. The fact is that winning customer loyalty today is harder than ever before. It takes more calls to find qualified prospects. It takes more callbacks to make individual sales, or more contacts or visits. It takes more service. This is why the majority of sales, and the largest purchases, from the most successful retailers and wholesalers come from repeat customers, not from first-time buyers.

The way that you generate repeat business is with high-quality products and outstanding customer service. The true measure of the success of your business is the percentage of your business that comes from repeat sales and referrals.

Where the Rubber Meets the Road

Your ability to actually *sell* the product, to convert the interested prospect into a confirmed customer, is where the rubber meets the road. It is another critical determinant of business success. Your ability to sell effectively flows from everything we have talked about in this program up until now.

Fortunately, all sales skills are *learnable*. You can learn any sales skill you need to learn to accomplish any sales goal you can set for yourself or for your business. There are no limits.

Selling is a simple, practical, proven process that has been learned and relearned hundreds of thousands of times by individuals and organizations. It can be learned and practiced by you so that your customers will say afterward: "This has been a great buying experience!"

When I started out in sales, I had no idea what I was doing. After working at laboring jobs for several years, and with no high school diploma, I got a job in straight commission sales, knocking on doors, cold-calling from dawn to dusk. I would start at 7:30 or 8:00 a.m., when people arrived at work, call on businesses all day, and then go out into the neighborhoods, calling on homes and apartments in the evenings. The only good news was that I was not afraid to work. I just wasn't making any sales.

After six months of fourteen-hour days, six days a week, barely making enough money to pay for one room in a small boarding house, I realized that a desire to be successful wasn't enough. I could barely sell anything. Finally, I did something that changed my life. I went to the most successful salesman in the company and asked him what he was doing differently from me that enabled him to sell five and ten times as much as anyone else.

He took me aside and went over my sales process with me, and showed me how to sell professionally. He told me the correct sequence of steps in a sales presentation, the questions to ask, and how to answer objections. He told me how to ask for the sale, and how to get referrals. And I did what he told me. And my sales went up, and up, and up!

What I learned, and what I subsequently relearned over the course of my business life, is that if you do what other successful people do, nothing can stop you from eventually getting the same results that they do. If you sell like other successful salespeople and companies sell, you will soon get the same results that they do. And if you don't, you won't.—Brian Tracy

A Doctor of Selling

Salespeople at every level should view themselves as "doctors of selling." This is a helpful model that is easy to teach and easy to learn.

If you go to a doctor of any kind, anywhere in the world, the doctor always follows an established procedure. It consists of three steps: examination, diagnosis, and recommended treatment or prescription. Salespeople should follow the same three-step model in their sales activities.

The Examination

Just as a doctor would insist upon doing a complete examination of the patient before drawing any conclusions or making any recommendations, you must do the same thing with each prospect.

Never assume that one size fits all. Never conclude that the reason someone else bought your product or service is identical to the reason that this person might buy your product or service. Before a great salesperson launches into her presentation, she listens to the customer carefully.

During the information-gathering process, discipline yourself to hold back from talking about your product or service, or making recommendations. A doctor would not start talking happily away about various pills that he might prescribe for a particular ailment before he had finished examining you. So, be patient. Ask a lot of questions. Do a thorough examination of the needs, wants, hopes, and desires of the customer.

The Diagnosis

In this stage, you take all of the information that the customer has given you and double-check it for accuracy by asking questions to test your understanding. You then share with the prospect what you believe his real want or need is, and how it could be satisfied.

Many patients do not have a clear understanding about their real problem or needs. This is why a good doctor will always explain his findings to you, explain the various courses of treatment available to you, and then recommend what might be the best treatment for you personally.

It is the physician's job, like the salesperson, to educate the patient about the various possibilities available. This process gives you credibility as a knowledgeable source of information and makes it clear that you have empathy for the customer's challenges. It opens the customer to listen to the range of solutions you are selling.

The Prescription

Only after you have done a thorough examination, and both discussed and agreed upon the diagnosis with the prospect, do you move to the third phase: the prescription or course of treatment. This is where you recommend the ideal product or service for this prospect, all things considered, and urge the prospect to take action.

A great insulation salesperson doesn't just show up to sell top-quality products and offer excellent prices. She first examines your house to understand how it is built and to find out how much you are currently paying in energy costs. She then shows you how you are spending twice as much as your neighbor on your energy bills because you have older insulation. She tells you about how your neighbors have fewer allergy symptoms because they don't have mildew in the attic from old insulation. She explains why your neighbor's house smells cleaner and fresher. She then recommends a course of action that you can take to install better insulation and get all the benefits that you have told her that you want.

Salespeople should consider themselves doctors of selling, as complete professionals who practice a craft, operate with a code of ethics, follow a set of procedures that work, and are completely devoted to the well-being of the customer (patient). This attitude of professionalism is practiced by the top 20 percent of sales professionals in every field.

Seven Rules for a Great Sales Process

Professional selling is an art and science, like cooking. Don't go into the kitchen without the following *seven* sacred ingredients. If you are lacking any one for your recipe, or if you mix them in the wrong order or proportion, the sale will not take place.

If you prefer, here's another analogy: Selling is like dialing a seven-digit telephone number. You must press each number in the proper sequence if you want to get through to the person at the other end of the line. In selling, you must follow this specific seven-step sales process to ensure the maximum number of sales, resales, and referrals.

Rule 1: Prospects versus Suspects

The first rule for sales success is "spend more time with better prospects." There may be many prospects for what you sell, but they are not all *your* prospects. We are cautioning you here about your sales process in the same way we did in Chapter 5 on marketing strategy. Most prospects are inappropriate for your company and your products and services.

Who are the primary buyers of your product or service? In most businesses, it is likely that less than 20 percent of your customers buy 80 percent of what you sell. You have to make it your business to find those customers who are the top 20 percent. If you are a discount stockbroker, you have to find the customers who trade the most. If you sell advertising, you have to find the clients who buy the most advertising.

It sounds obvious, but many business owners behave as if they have no idea who their best customers are. We are amazed at how often we go into companies where they have done extensive research in the marketing department, but nevertheless the sales group ends up wasting time and money shooting in all directions. Get your customer service people and your marketing team and your sales force all together to talk about the best buyers in your market.

Your first job is to separate prospects from "suspects." Take your time and ask questions. Your sales energies and resources are limited. You cannot waste them by spending too much time with people who either cannot or will not buy.

A good prospect has qualities that fall into several categories:

- **Timing.** The prospect has a genuine need that your product or service can satisfy, and he has that need now.

- **Problem.** The prospect has a clear, identifiable problem that your product or service can solve.

- **Value.** The prospect has a clear goal that your product or service will help him to achieve at a cost that is clearly less than the value of the goal itself.

- **Pain.** Your prospect is dissatisfied or has discontent of some kind that your product or service can take away.

- **Result.** The prospect has a definite result that he wants or needs to accomplish, and your product or service will help him to achieve that result faster, better, and cheaper than he could in the absence of what you are selling.

In every case, the most important factor is *clarity*. Both you and the prospect need to be completely clear that the need, problem, goal, result, or pain exists and that your product or service is a cost-effective way of dealing with it.

Rule 2: Establishing Rapport and Trust

Despite all the data and expertise invested in the sales process, the vast majority of buying decisions end up being made on the basis of *emotion,* especially about how buyers (or their peers) feel about the product and the salesperson. How buyers feel about the salesperson extends to how they feel about the entire company.

The best sales process is one in which you educate consumers about the problems they face—with great factual detail— and then demonstrate the benefits provided by solutions you are selling. However, the biggest part of the sale goes on after the sale.

Once you have made the sale, you must deliver the product or service, make sure that it is satisfactorily installed and utilized, and take care of customer concerns or complaints for a substantial time afterward. That is why the customer wants a relationship first. As far as the customer is concerned, the relationship with the salesperson can become more important than the product or service you are selling.

There is a "law of indirect effort" in selling. It says that the more you focus on the relationship (the indirect approach), the more the sale will take care of itself. But the more you focus on the sale, ignoring the relationship, the less likely it is that you will achieve either a sale or a good customer relationship.

The most important elements in a sales relationship are trust and credibility. The customer must trust you (the salesperson) completely and have complete confidence that you will fulfill your promises. The customer must believe that your product or service will do what you say it will do, and continue doing it.

Telling is not selling. There is a direct relationship between the number of questions you ask about the customer's wants and needs, and the strength of the relationship that you form. Telling is not selling. Only asking is selling.

In addition, there is a direct relationship between how carefully you listen to the customer's answers, and how much the customer likes and trusts you. The fact is that *listening builds trust.* There is no faster or more effective way to build a high trust relationship between the salesperson and the customer than for the salesperson to ask lots of questions and listen carefully to the answers.

The more closely you listen to the customer when he speaks, the more he will like and trust you and be open to buying your product or service. Questions are the key and trust is the essential factor.

Rule 3: Identifying Needs Accurately

Many customers do not know that they have a need that your product or service can satisfy when they first talk to you. In their minds, they are tire kickers; that is, they are simply gathering information.

When you speak to a customer, he may have a need that is *clear, unclear,* or *nonexistent.* If the need is clear, the customer may be accurate or inaccurate about how to satisfy that need. Maybe what he needs is very different from what he thinks he needs.

If the need is unclear, it is only through the examination and diagnosis process that you and the customer become clear on exactly what need exists and how it can best be satisfied with what you offer.

In many cases, the customer may think that he has a need, but his situation is really satisfactory as it is. He does not need your product or service, and it is your duty as a professional to tell him that.

The way you identify needs accurately is by asking questions, from the general to the particular, and listening to the answers. This is why the highest paid salespeople prepare their questions carefully in advance, writing them down, and asking them in sequence.

The worst salespeople say whatever falls out of their mouth and lurch back and forth through the sales conversation like a drunk staggering from lamppost to lamppost. A disjointed questioning process invariably lowers credibility and makes the sale increasingly difficult to achieve.

Rule 4: Presenting Persuasively

The presentation is where the actual sale is made. You can make a lot of mistakes in the sales process, but the quality of your presentation determines whether or not the customer buys.

The best sales method is to *show, tell, and ask a question.* For example, you say: "This is a small business accounting software program. With it, you can manage all the numbers in your business. Is this something that would be of interest to you?"

Use the "trial close" throughout your presentation. This is a closing question that can be answered with a "no" without stopping the sales process, because it allows the salesperson another opportunity to respond. For example:

Salesperson: Would you want to install this software on your home office computer?

Customer: No. I would rather use it in my office downtown.

Salesperson: No problem. It works equally well on either home computer or server operating systems.

In addition, a powerful and professional sales presentation is one that continually refers to other customers who have used the product or service successfully in the past. Tell stories about other customers who are in the same or a similar situation as this prospect, but who bought the product or service and were happy as a result.

Rule 5: Answering Objections Effectively

There are no sales without objections. Objections indicate interest. The more the prospect questions you about your product or service, the more likely it is that she is interested enough to buy it.

The "law of six" applies to objections. It says that there are never more than six objections to any product or service offering. Sometimes there are only one or two, but never more than six. Your job is to sit down with a sheet of paper and write out the answer to the question: "What are all the reasons that a qualified prospect might give me for not buying my product or service?"

Even if you receive dozens of objections in the course of a week or a month, they can all be clustered around no more than six categories. Your job is to identify the major objections that you are likely to get and then to develop bulletproof, logical answers to each of those objections so that they do not stop the sales process.

Rule 6: Closing the Sale

In golf, they say, "You drive for show, but you putt for dough."

In sales, you follow every step we have talked about up until now, but your ability to close the sale and to get the prospect to make a buying decision is where you "putt for dough."

The most powerful word in the sales process is "ask." Most people are terrified of rejection, of being told "no" in a sales conversation. For this reason, they don't ask at all. They sit there passively and hope the customer will take the initiative and buy their product or service. But this seldom happens. Even if the customer wants the product, needs it, can use it, and can afford it, the responsibility of the sales person is to reach out verbally and ask for a buying decision.

Making an invitational close. Perhaps the simplest of all closing techniques is the *invitational close*. After you have made a presentation, you ask: "Do you have any questions or concerns that I haven't covered so far?"

When the customer says, "No, I think you've covered everything," you then roll into an invitational close by saying, "Well, then, why don't you give it a try?"

Alternatively, you could talk about how they would like the product or service delivered.

Many customers are only one question away from buying. All they need is a little nudge or encouragement. When you ask, "If you like it, why don't you give it a try?" you will be amazed at how many people say, "Sure, why not?"

The good news is that if you have built a high level of rapport and trust, identified needs accurately, made a clear benefit-oriented presentation, and answered any objections the prospect has, the closing of the sale follows naturally. It is simple and easy and almost foreordained. You must never be afraid to ask.

Rule 7: Getting Resales and Referrals

This is the most important part of the sales process. Everything must be aimed at taking such good care of your customer that he buys from you again and recommends you to his friends and associates. Treat him like a *million-dollar customer*, as if he had the ability to purchase enormous quantities of your product and to recommend you to a substantial number of other prospects.

On average, a person knows 300 people by their first names. They can be friends, relatives, teachers and classmates, coworkers or other job-related contacts, and associates of all kinds, such as your banker or accountant.

Imagine that only 10 percent of the people whom one of your customers knows are prospective customers for your products or services as well. This would mean that each person who buys from you has the potential to bring you *thirty* additional customers, if you treat your current customer really well. Each of those thirty additional customers also knows 300 people. And approximately 10 percent of those additional people can buy from you as well.

This means that each person that you sell to can potentially bring you 900 (30 x 30) prospects in the months ahead. Does that get your attention? Does that have an effect on the way you treat the individual customer standing in front of you? We hope so.

Selling to a referral takes one-fifteenth of the time, money, and energy required to sell to a cold-call or a new customer. In consumer retailing, for example, when someone is referred to you by a happy customer, that person is 95 percent sold before she's even contacted you for the first time. Word-of-mouth is extraordinarily powerful in growing your business if you can tap into it on a regular and systematic basis.

Asking for referrals. The key to getting referrals is to "be referable." Give such good service and educational information to the customer that he feels confident recommending you to his friends, family, and associates. When you take good care of your customers, they will want their friends to enjoy the same experience.

Be sure to ask for referrals at every opportunity. You can say, "Mr. Prospect, I really like working with people like you. Do you know any other *great people* like yourself who might be interested in my product or service?"

Who is going to tell you that they don't know any other *great people?*

When you get a referral from a happy customer to a new prospect, be sure to report back to the customer and share exactly what happened. People are inordinately curious about what you did and said to their friends or associates, and how they responded.

When you make a sale to a referral, send a thank-you letter or, even better, a gift to the source of the referral. My favorite choice is a gift basket with delicious foods of some kind. People always like to receive gifts, and they will be much more likely to give you more referrals in the future if you show your appreciation.

There are many books, articles, CDs, and sales training programs that expand on these seven steps in the sales process. What's especially important to know is that sometimes, a small improvement in any one area can lead to a dramatic improvement in your success.

Six Elements of Mega-Credibility in Selling

Today, it takes credibility for you to get a hearing with a prospect, but it takes mega-credibility for you to get the sale. There are six elements of mega-credibility you can develop and use in your sales activities:

1. Your market visibility
2. Your company
3. Testimonials
4. Professional presentation
5. Your salesperson
6. The product itself

Your Visibility in the Market

Few things are more effective in building credibility than to be a "known quantity" in your business. The best sales organizations are intimately tied into the activities of the press organizations that specialize in their industry. They know the top reporters and editors. They make presentations at all the key trade shows. They become valued volunteer officers of the right professional associations. They participate in their professional service organizations and the community organizations that give them visibility. They know the analysts who write research reports, the columnists who specialize in their industry, and the bloggers who cover their market. They write their own blogs and newsletters, helping to educate customers in the marketplace.

Who are the people who "influence" your clients most? Who are the thought leaders they look to for advice and insights? What publications and/or thought leaders do your prospects pay the most attention to? Who has the most impact on public opinion about your product or service?

Your Company

Your company has three elements that build credibility: its *size, reputation,* and *longevity.* With regard to size, the bigger a company is, the more it is assumed to be offering a high-quality product or service. Why else would so many people buy so much of it?

If you don't have size going for you, then you need to compensate with other creative and useful features that make your offering better. As a small businessperson, you must demonstrate that big is not always better—your small business provides more specialized or more personal and attentive service, for instance.

The longevity of your company could make its products more trustworthy. There is a natural assumption that if your company is large, has a good reputation, and has been in business for a long time, it must be selling high-quality products and services that are obviously worth more than those sold by newer or lesser known companies.

The reputation of a company is extremely important, perhaps more than any other factor, in building mega-credibility. One of the most powerful trust-building actions a salesperson can take is to mention how large the company is *and* how respected it is in the industry. Never assume that your prospective customers have any knowledge about your company when they first talk to you.

Testimonials

Testimonials are a great way to demonstrate and promote your reputation in the market with your prospects. After all, one of the most common, though sometimes unspoken questions that every customer has is: "Who else has bought your product or service?"

There is nothing that builds the credibility of a product, service, or company faster than the knowledge that lots of people, hundreds or thousands, have already bought the product or service, with satisfactory results.

Be sure to tell the prospect how many people have already bought this product or service and are currently enjoying it. Share with the prospective customer testimonial letters from your existing customers. Show the customer lists of other people who have bought the product or service. Show the customer photographs of other customers using or enjoying the product or service you are selling. Shoot video testimonials from happy customers and play them for your prospect on your laptop.

The use of testimonials is one of the fastest and most powerful ways to build the mega-credibility you need to make the sale.

Professional Presentation

Your sales presentation must be thorough, prepared, and customized for this prospect. By some estimates, you can increase the perceived value of a product or service by two or three times by the simple act of presenting it professionally. That means doing careful preparation in advance and learning everything you can about the customer. You plan your presentation thoroughly, in every detail. You make your presentation smoothly and fluently, answering each of the customer's questions or concerns. A professional sales presentation—customized for your specific client's needs and challenges—significantly lowers fear and skepticism and raises trust and credibility.

Your Salesperson

The quality, character, and confidence of the salesperson have a huge influence on the sales result, and they are conveyed, variously, by the salesperson's conduct and appearance, knowledge, and attitude.

■ **Conduct and Appearance.** It's difficult to build a relationship with your customers if they are uncomfortable with you from the moment you meet them. Do you know how to behave appropriately with your prospects? Do you speak your customer's language? Do you understand their culture and customs? Do you dress for success so that you are taken seriously in the customer's organization?

It is absolutely essential that salespeople study proper conduct, behavior, and dress for the business, organization, or individual to whom they are selling. The rule is, "If it doesn't help, it hurts." Everything counts.

■ **Knowledge.** The best salespeople learn every possible detail they can about the customer's business before they meet with the customer for the first time. They research and think through how the customer can most benefit from what they are selling. The more you can demonstrate genuine interest and value-added knowledge about how the product or service will be used, the more powerful an impact you will have on the prospect.

While there is much truth to the notion that a talented salesperson can "sell anything" to anyone, the greatest salespeople generally care enough about the customer and the product to become an expert. They are genuinely concerned about their customers and want to help them to solve their problems and achieve their goals.

■ **Attitude.** Top salespeople love and enjoy the product they sell. They like to talk about it and explain it to others, especially customers. They want to learn more about their product and what it can do for their customers. People who love their

Authenticity or Arrogance?

Many people try to express their individuality by using humor or gestures, or by dressing or grooming themselves in a way that draws attention to them. While you might sincerely be trying to be authentic and to "be yourself" (and your heart is in the right place), customers or their organizational culture may not appreciate it. They may not understand your intentions. They may see your lack of sensitivity to their sensibilities as arrogance, or worse.

It *is* arrogant not to do your homework first. You need to show respect in a way that doesn't compromise who you are. That means understanding everything you can about the world your customer lives in.

For guidance on proper appearance and conduct, study the most successful salespeople in your field. They are not all the same either in terms of background, temperament, or personality. How are they reaching out to prospects in ways that honestly win the trust of their customers? Follow their lead; harvest their insights. Get in step with your customer.

work and think it matters will learn twice as much and work twice as hard as those who don't.

The Product Itself

The final element for building mega-credibility is an ability to demonstrate to the customer that your product or service is the

The Three P's of High Performance

In our research for *Success Built to Last*, we studied people who were high achievers for at least twenty years— from billionaires to Nobel Laureates. Despite their field or profession, we found they have three traits in common that are difficult for a leader to fake: *passion, purpose*, and *performance*. They love what they do (passion) and think that it is important to customers (purpose). When they are clear about their passion and purpose, they become intensely result and action oriented (performance).

When all three traits are combined in your sales work, you'll win sales time after time. When you take the time to learn about your customers' passions, purpose, and performance, you will bond with them. Customers will enjoy being with you and feel confident buying from you.

ideal one for him at this time, and that your price is reasonable and fair, relative to the value that the customer receives. Having the right product for the right customer at the right time and at the right price is the ultimate test of credibility.

The Ultimate Test

In the final analysis, your ability to convert interested prospects into buying customers is the critical measure that determines success or failure. Top companies of all sizes see themselves as "sales organizations." The top people think about customers and sales all day long. The best salespeople are the highest paid and most respected people in the organization.

In sales, remember that *you become successful when you give success to others.* If your financial results are not what you want today, put everything else aside and get out there and talk to buyers. Partner with your customers and commit to helping them achieve their goals. Sell something you really believe in that provides lasting value to customers, and they'll reward you by sending money right back in your door. And never give up!

CHAPTER 6 CHECKLIST FOR PERFECTING A GREAT SALES PROCESS

1. Identify the three most important **factors that influence and determine the success** of salespeople in your company or industry:

   a. _____

   b. _____

   c. _____

2. List three actions you could take immediately to **attract more and better prospects** to your business:

   a. _____

   b. _____

   c. _____

3. What are the three most important **sales skills** that you and your salespeople need to excel in to achieve your sales goals?

    a. _____

    b. _____

    c. _____

4. List three things you could do immediately to build **higher levels of trust** and mega-credibility with your prospects and customers?

    a. _____

    b. _____

    c. _____

5. What three actions could your salespeople take to make **more persuasive and effective sales presentations**?

    a. _____

    b. _____

    c. _____

6. What three actions could you take, or incentives could you offer, **to get your prospects to buy sooner** rather than delaying a purchase decision?

    a. _____

    b. _____

    c. _____

7. List three questions that you could ask to **elicit a buying decision** from an interested prospect:

   a. _____

   b. _____

   c. _____

   What **one action** are you going to take immediately to increase your sales?

   _____

   _____

   _____

Create a Great Customer Experience

"The golden rule for every businessman is this: 'Put yourself in your customer's place.'"

—ORISON SWETT MARDEN

T he secret to success in business can be summarized in a single sentence: "Make your customers happy."

The key to your business future is the degree to which you create that experience for people—that you delight customers over and over again and make them happy that they decided to do business with you.

Nothing generates greater customer satisfaction, loyalty,

and repeat business more than a companywide commitment to pleasing your customers. It is the key to triggering the response, "This is a great company!"

It is expensive to acquire a customer for the first time. Once you have a customer, you must do everything possible to "bind him to you with hoops of steel." Develop an obsession with customer service. Take care of your customers better than your competitors and continually look for ways to improve.

Your aim should be to get your customers selling for you. You want your customers to "go viral" and infect the market with your message. You want them telling their colleagues and neighbors about your company. You want your customers to be sending e-mails and blogging about your products and services to each other.

Twelve Steps to the Ultimate Customer Experience

The starting point of developing an excellent customer service policy is to define how you intend to treat your customers. Start by defining the "ultimate customer experience."

If the customer experience were perfect, what would happen? If your customers could say anything to other people about your services, what would you want them to say?

At the Stanford University Real-time Venture Design Lab, we studied why the vast majority of start-ups fail quickly. We assembled venture capitalists, experienced entrepreneurs, psychologists, sociologists, even *narratologists*—experts who study the impact of stories on the core beliefs and behaviors in many cultures.

We scoured piles of research on the topic and interrogated the founding members of new start-ups that had been operating for less than a year, as well as those firms that had been successful for decades. We watched customers and stakeholders use the products or services of these companies and talked about what mattered to them. We found twelve factors that give insight into the ultimate customer experience:

1. Reliability and Consistency: Be Predictable

How would you feel if every time you met your friends they were different? Imagine how difficult it would be for you to keep those relationships if every time you saw them they had changed their appearance, voice, and manner. (Although if you've ever lived in New York City or San Francisco, as Mark has for many years, you may find that happens more often than you'd like!)

That is precisely how jarring and unnerving it feels to customers when you change your product too often without a good reason. Schwab.com always wanted to improve its website every time the company got a new idea, but customers often hated the unfamiliar changes more than they appreciated the "improvements" that Schwab was so excited about. Many websites routinely change their navigation, for example, just as customers have learned to use and enjoy it—leaving them feeling lost again.

When Coke infamously came out with "New Coke," its market share plummeted. A century of success was nearly destroyed by impatience and an intrinsic need for change for its own sake, not the customer's sake. Today, the Coca-Cola Company experiments with and *adds* hundreds of flavors to meet changing local tastes, but it never changes the original Coca-Cola formula.

Reliability and consistency means customers can count on the brand to mean the same thing every time they experience the product or service—like McDonald's, KFC, or Domino's Pizza. You know exactly how they will taste every time you purchase their products. For most companies, that's the definition of a brand.

2. Responsibility: Raise Your Hand When You Make a Mistake

Study after study shows that when most customers complain, they don't really want their money back or to cancel the purchase. They just want the product to work. They want the company that sold the product to fulfill the promises made when it made the sale.

People don't expect you to be perfect. What they expect is for you to take responsibility for the good and bad things that happen when the customer experiences your product. It is amazing how many companies (along with celebrities and politicians) are forgiven of something if they commit to action, quickly apologize, and take responsibility.

When you make a mistake of any kind, immediately apologize and move quickly to solve the problem. Refuse to make excuses or to blame someone or something else. Take action to take care of the customer.

There can be good news in bad news. Ironically, an error gives you an invitation to dig deeper and have a more meaningful conversation with your customer than ever before. Your most loyal customers may come as a result of your mistakes. When a customer complained about an allergic episode that she thought she had while staying at a Marriott hotel, the manager saw an opportunity to show off something that most customers don't usually think about: the hotel's scrupulously detailed cleaning process for every room. That is something that a customer would normally never hear about.

In this case, the customer was so impressed that she traded up to a Marriott timeshare, spending tens of thousands of dollars because she was now convinced that she could trust the hotel chain to do much more than its competitors.

Increasing loyalty. A customer who complains and receives a fast response will actually be more loyal to the company in terms of future sales and referrals than a customer who never complained at all.

On the other hand, a slow response to a customer complaint triggers fear and anger. The customer is afraid that he is going to be stuck with a product that doesn't work and feels angry that he went ahead with the purchase in the first place.

The rule is to respond quickly to customer complaints; refuse to defend or make excuses and offer to make the customer happy immediately. Be open and honest in all your dealings with your customers. Assume that anything you do or say will become public knowledge quickly. Tell the truth and tell it as soon as you know it. Resolve to build and maintain trust in everything you do.

3. Responsiveness: Get in Front of the Story Fast

When your spouse or significant other asks, "Do you love me?," it's not just important to answer affirmatively. You had better answer *fast*! Speed matters.

Today, with instantaneous and global communication, consumers flash text messages about your product that make minutes count. The longer Toyota remained in denial about the acceleration problem in certain of its vehicles in 2010, the bigger the crisis became—and the longer it will take the company to repair its reputation.

United Airlines is finding it hard to live down the story about baggage handlers destroying a passenger's prized musical instrument while the whole plane watched. Millions of dollars in PR damage could have been avoided by spending $3,500 to replace a customer's cherished Taylor guitar. But the airline didn't budge. Dave Carroll and his band, Sons of Maxwell, found sweet revenge in a music video called "United Breaks Guitars," a parody of Carroll's experience, which generated more than 8 million views with over 42,000 five-star ratings on YouTube. United was almost twittered to death with bad press, while the band's career was catapulted to new heights.

Everyone should be clear that the customer is the person who determines your success or failure in your job—and your paycheck. Sam Walton once said, "We all have one boss, and that is the customer. And he can fire us at any time by simply choosing to buy somewhere else."

You are the advocate for your customer. Think of yourself as the consumer protection agency for your best customers. Be sure to constantly reevaluate the rewards and recognition system to make sure you have the right incentives for your team. You need alignment with your customers to stay deeply committed to great customer service, and that means providing clear disincentives for poor performance.

To win in a competitive market, you must demonstrate deep empathy for the trials, tribulations, and triumphs of your customer. Every customer contact is a "moment of truth." It has an impact on the customer and, by extension, an impact on the future of your business. You have heard the old saying, *They don't care how much you know until they know how much you care.* Your job is to remind customers continually that you appreciate them.

4. Specialized Service: Make It Feel Like a Custom Fit

Is your customer experience what the buyer really wants? Are you a specialist in the customer's unique needs? How can you put your company in a position to provide a unique customer experience that competitors can't match without great sacrifice to their other customers?

One company has been able to provide a specialized service so well that more customers are willing to recommend its brand and repurchase the product than any other, according to the *BusinessWeek*/J. D. Powers survey of Customer Service Champs in 2010. It's USAA, the insurance company, and it did it by focusing on a niche with an unmet need. USAA's market is U.S. military officers who couldn't get auto insurance—due to the perception that they were high risk. Of the top ten automobile insurance competitors, USAA is the only provider that restricts service to members, and their families, of the United States military.

Just-in-time customer experiences. The University of Phoenix is another specialist that makes its user experience feel customized for more than 400,000 enrolled students—making it the biggest college in the world. The company's parent, Apollo Group, saw revenues grow 27 percent in 2009—to $4 billion—while most educational institutions suffered in the economic downturn. Why?

"The university was among the first to *come to the customer* rather than the other way around," said University of Phoenix's George Lichter. "We didn't focus on real estate—a pretentious campus setting or snob appeal." Instead, they get right down to business with a practical college degree for working professionals that is available 24/7, exactly when and how their customers want it. Most traditional colleges, on the other hand, still refuse to think of their students as customers.

"Our campuses don't have ivy or a quadrangle in the center, but our classes are online on your desktop, or conveniently within fifteen or twenty miles of 70 percent of Americans," Lichter said.

Even more important, the University of Phoenix discovered it "had more in common with HBO—the cable company—than it did with Harvard," Lichter added. Cable companies long ago realized they not only were distributing other people's content, but they were a distribution platform, which meant they could produce their own TV shows. And since they knew the customer better than the networks or the studios, they could therefore customize programs for viewers.

The University of Phoenix, unlike traditional educational institutions, has similar advantages. It is able to create just that right coursework, in just the right way and at the right time, for its customers.

Some services always feel personal. When Mark bought the wrong electric mower at Home Depot online, he was able to return it stress free to any Home Depot store. Home Depot has done something many companies haven't. It makes it easy for customers to move between its retail locations and the online site. That's something that every customer wants. Home Depot's policy gives buyers much more confidence about buying anything, anytime, from the store or the website. It builds trust and loyalty.

5. Selection: Be Sure to Have the Product Available

To elicit the response you want from your customers and to have them say, "This is a great product," you have to have it in stock. When Mark discovered he bought the wrong mower—and found it so easy to return it to his local Home Depot store—he naturally wanted to buy the *right* electric mower from them. Unfortunately, the store didn't have it in inventory in December. Granted, not a lot of folks mow lawns during the holidays. But lawns still grow in California in the winter and, believe it or not, it was a Christmas present. (His father-in-law really did want a cordless electric mower.) The helpful staff searched other stores in the area, which was another great service, but to no avail. They recommended HomeDepot.com, which strangely didn't offer the item online in December, either.

In the end, Mark found the mower he was searching for and bought it (for even less) at Amazon.com. It was kind of a shame, don't you think? Home Depot deserved that sale from a loyal customer. The company gave great service when the wrong product had to be returned. But ultimately it didn't have the right product when the customer needed it.

It's an expensive balancing act to have just the right inventory at the right time and not break your bank account, whether you're a small or big business. Inventory costs money and creates risk if it's not sold. But in terms of providing a great customer experience, you need to find a way to deliver when the customer wants to buy it.

6. Quality: It's Defined by Your Customer

Quality is defined as the suitability of the product or service to the customer's special and unique situation. Quality means that your product or service conforms (and hopefully exceeds) the customer's standards and requirements.

There are different bands or strata of quality. In mass-market retailing, companies like Wal-Mart, Costco, and Best Buy continue to gain market share because they've matched product performance and service with their customer segments. They don't always have the swankiest or highest end stuff, but they do provide what their specific customers expect for the price.

During World War II, thousands of men trained to be paratroopers, but on too many occasions the parachutes did not open during the trial jumps. Fortunately, the paratroopers wore double parachutes so the level of fatalities in training was very low. However, no matter how often the parachute packers were admonished or offered bonuses and rewards for packing the parachutes properly, the default level of parachutes that failed to open remained unacceptably high.

Finally, one of the officers came up with an idea. He announced to the parachute packers that the next morning they would all be taken up to an altitude of 5,000 feet and forced to jump with one of the parachutes they had personally packed. Not surprisingly, every single parachute opened perfectly during this trial jump.

The officer then gathered the parachute packers together and said that, from now on, on a random basis, the parachute packers would be taken up and forced to jump with a parachute chosen at random from the ones they had packed in the previous week. From that moment on, every parachute was packed perfectly and there was never again an incident of a parachute not opening in use.

7. Delivery: Exceed Expectations as Often as Possible

It's no surprise that companies that offer fast, dependable, predictable delivery of their products attract business away from suppliers whose delivery is slow or inconsistent. Zappos.com, the online vendor of shoes, grew from an idea for fast and imaginative customer service to a billion-dollar company in nine years. According to the company's CEO, the joke that customers tell is that "as soon as you submit your order online with Zappos.com, you have to get up and hurry to the front door because the shoes you just ordered will be delivered so fast."

The day Mark met Tony Hsieh, founder and CEO of Zappos, the company was celebrating an employee who was being recognized for achieving a company record for the longest phone conversation with a customer. It was about five hours. Wait a minute—if you are like us, you probably thought call centers were supposed to be measured by how fast employees can close the sale and get off the phone! That's a very common measure in most companies, but not Zappos. The company determined that repeat sales were a better measure, and as a result, no other major shoe distribution company is growing faster.

8. Employee Experience: Make Your People Feel Happy About Working for You

Entrepreneurs like Zappos founder Tony Hsieh understand that if you make your people feel important, that is exactly how they will make your customers feel.

When you take a tour of the Zappos offices, you will see for yourself. It is well worth a lunch hour to do so if you are in Las Vegas. You'll see wacky outfits and wild-looking cubicles decorated in themes that range from Animal House to Wizard of Oz. On the day of our visit, Hsieh himself was hanging out in a little cubicle with a jungle growing over his head, a stuffed monkey and peanut shells on the floor. You can almost walk by without noticing him.

Employees in each row of cubicles ring a bell, applaud, and celebrate as touring guests pass by. The company's chief coach, Dr. Vic, has a *throne* for guests who visit his office. He offers you a paper crown, then photographs you as royalty, then gives you a Polaroid print. Some great companies put employees on a pedestal, but not literally. Dr. Vic is one of the few folks with a private office at Zappos, and his wallpaper is made of 1,500 of photos of his favorite people: the entire Zappos team.

You'll find Hsieh's favorite business books framed in the hallways, and he encourages everyone to read them, offering free copies in the lobby. (The wall hangings included, to our delight, *Success Built to Last*.) Realizing who Mark was, the Zappos team naturally asked him to compete with the tour guide in a hula-hoop contest. (Mark broke all records in his age category, but fell well short of the score of our twenty-year-old instructor.)

9. Commitment by Employees: Make Them Love It or Leave It

When you've completed your employee training at Zappos, you're asked to leave. That's right. They offer you a check for $2,000 to buzz off.

Only a tiny fraction of the people take the bait.

The key to an extraordinary customer experience is to make sure the people on your team who don't want to be there go somewhere else. Sounds harsh, but it isn't. They ought to leave at the earliest opportunity. They're better off and so are you. They can then focus on doing something that they like, and you can focus on your customers.

What you want are people who say, every day, "*This* is a great place to work."

10. Installation: Make Everything Work for Your Customer

Best Buy has revolutionized the retail electronics industry by sending out its Geek Squad in nerdy black-and-white Volkswagens to make house calls. Once on-site, these technicians integrate in-home consumer electronic products (e.g., computers, network routers, entertainment systems) so they actually work together as one neat package. What a concept! They make the installation of these various systems secure, worry-free, and time-saving for consumers, which is a departure from the way electronics manufacturers themselves work (they actually don't

NOW, BUILD A GREAT BUSINESS!

want their equipment to work with their competitor's products; they want you to buy only their products).

When Best Buy realized it wasn't just a retail store, it became a trusted service provider—surmounting the installation conundrum for customers in a high-tech world where most consumer electronics are sold to primarily nontechnical people. Customers may not have known that they wanted an extra service of this kind, but once they discovered it, they wanted it by, well, yesterday! Customers today are more impatient than ever. Instant gratification is no longer fast enough. Any business that offers to serve its customers faster immediately becomes the preferred supplier, even at a higher price.

11. Context: Find Out How It Feels to Be a Customer

When crime was wildly out of control on the New York City subway system, the only way to get officials to take action was to have the Commissioner require the senior team to actually ride the subway for themselves. Horrified, they finally understood the customer experience.

Context is king. There's nothing more powerful in business than context. When you see a product or service in action (and inaction), you will learn more than you would with a million phone surveys.

Mark worked for Schwab.com when it was growing into the world's largest financial services website, and he would bring Schwab product managers into a dimly lit room with a one-way mirror as if they were going to pick out suspects in a criminal line-up. It's called a usability lab. On the other side of the mirror was a lone customer sitting at a PC. The managers would watch customers try to navigate the website *without help*. You could see the screen of the computer and the pained expression on the client's face.

The client's suffering is not the customer's fault, it's yours.

Customer Intimacy

When Schwab asked clients about its online services, they would say that it was better than others, but they hated how difficult it was to use. Being the best in a crummy category isn't a safe place to rest on your laurels.

But when Schwab product managers could see and feel *firsthand* in the usability lab just how hard it was for clients to find things or figure them out, their attitude changed. They saw one customer after another face one frustration after another. It was heartbreaking for them to witness the challenges that Schwab.com's navigation posed for clients.

After watching a dozen customers struggle with navigating his product page on the website, one Schwab product manager pounded on the glass and said, "It's not in the left corner, you idiot!" He shouted and pointed at the computer screen. "It's on the right side on the top!"

Thank goodness the client couldn't hear the outburst. And, yes, Schwab fired [that manager] soon afterward."
—Mark Thompson

12. Competition: *Be* the Customer

Most business leaders sit at their desks and say they are customer focused, but you usually can't get a full flavor for the customer when you are sitting in the office. You have to get out and into the trenches with your customer.

There is a simple but powerful exercise that you can do within your company on a regular basis: Require everyone on your team to buy from your successful competitors. Visit their places of business, read their advertisements, and look at what they promise to their customers. You don't need to reinvent the wheel. Sometimes, you can get wonderful ideas to improve your customer service experience simply by being inspired or dismayed by your successful competitors, and then doing them one better.

Reward your team for insight. Recognize your team every time they bring a specific experience back from using the competitors' services. In a surprising number of companies, managers aren't allowed to use the other guy's products. Or if they do, it's only politically correct to report a complaint about the competitors' shortcomings. This is self-delusion and often a missed opportunity to find a way to improve your own customer services.

That's the problem with the customer experience. It rarely happens at your desk. It demands that you and your team leave the conference room and set aside the spreadsheets and strategy sessions and go out and experience exactly what the customer experiences—not with insiders or handlers who explain it or dress it up for you in staff meetings. You have to go out there alone and be a customer.

As star venture capitalist Mike Maples says, "You can make ungrounded assertions all night long about what you think is going on with customers, but the facts you're looking for are never in the building with you."

What Should You Be Doing More of?

Analyze the behaviors and activities your customers appreciate most and for which you receive the greatest number of compliments. Build on success. Whenever you get positive feedback from customers for any reason, take it seriously. Look around and see if you cannot repeat that behavior or action with other customers.

What Should You Be Doing Less of?

You should reduce, cut back, or eliminate activities or behaviors that customers either do not like or do not want. It is amazing how many companies offer services to customers that they don't really care about, while diverting their resources away from services that customers really want. This is often the hardest thing to do unless your business is in a crisis.

Letting Go: Practice Creative Abandonment

At every stage of business development, a company must be prepared to start new things and stop old things. Peter Drucker calls this the process of "creative abandonment."

Your time, money, and resources are *limited*. To start something new, you probably have to discontinue something that's old and less effective. One of the very best ways to simplify and streamline operations in your business is to eliminate any and all activities that are not leading to higher levels of customer satisfaction.

Practice *zero-based thinking* in everything you do. Continually ask, "Is there anything we are doing today that, knowing what we now know, we would not start up again today if we had to do it over?"

Would You Do It Again?

In every business, and in every career, there are answers to this question. In times of turbulence and rapid change, there will always be activities that you need to discontinue altogether, activities that are no longer valuable to today's customers in today's markets.

You should also ask, "Are there any products or services that we are offering today that, knowing what we now know, we would not bring to the market today if we had it to do over?" The vast majority of products and services developed and sold in competitive markets will eventually fail and will need to be discontinued or eliminated. If customers are not buying your product or service in sufficient quantities, at satisfactory prices, and you cannot improve them to make them competitive, they are excellent candidates for discontinuation.

Does It Work?

It takes tremendous courage to admit that something that seemed like a good idea at the time has turned out to be a poor idea. It's even worse when you have invested in a process that doesn't work for your customer. But the only question you should ask, over and over, is: Does it work?

The rule is to try, try again, and then try something else. Don't fall in love with an idea, product, or service. Don't pave the cow path! The market is a stern taskmaster, but you must let the market be the judge. Very often, a product or service that was ideal at one time becomes no longer attractive or competitive. The market changes, customer preferences change, and that's when it is time to cut your losses and move on.

Customer Satisfaction Isn't Enough

As a rule, you should treat every customer as though you were on the verge of losing that customer every single day. Continually seek ways to improve the quality of the customer experience in dealing with your company. Never be satisfied. Keep raising the bar.

"Customer satisfaction isn't enough," according to bestselling business author Jason Jennings. "Customers who say they're only *satisfied* on surveys are the ones who leave at the first opportunity and go elsewhere. You have to exceed expectations if you want loyalty."

Creating an Extraordinary Customer Experience

If you want to enjoy one of the ultimate retail customer service experiences, visit the Four Seasons restaurant in Manhattan. You won't be surprised that it is also rated as one of the best culinary experiences in the world. The soaring spaces, exotic aromas, and sharp waiting staff instantly impress you. But what is really extraordinary is how hard they work at making each and every guest feel comfortable in a relaxed and professional way.

Alex von Bidder, the soft-spoken Swiss co-owner of the Four Seasons, approaches you in his elegant hand-tailored suit with his hand extended. He moves with such grace and warmth that he's been called the Fred Astaire of the restaurant business. He enjoys choreographing his team and is intimately involved with making the customer experience better every week.

Elegant but Down-to-Earth

While von Bidder is accustomed to serving the rich and famous, there's something downright earthy about him. There's nothing fake, and you can feel an open-hearted earnestness in his voice. He knows that the first impression is critical, but it's not enough.

"The best customer experience makes you feel welcome and special enough to come back," von Bidder whispered as he walked us to the table. He seemed to bow as he pulled out a chair next to the lighted fountain in the center of the room. It's obvious that this fellow loves this place and he's genuinely delighted that you are visiting his home.

"If you want a spectacular customer experience, you have to find people who love that experience as much as you do. Once you're sure a waiter can provide for your guests exquisitely, then you have to let them be who they are as individuals. No one wants a relationship with a machine or a snob. Excellent service always feels personal."

Four Levels of Customer Satisfaction

There are four different levels of customer satisfaction that may be achieved by your business. If you don't achieve these levels, your competitors will soon do it, and take away your customers.

1. **Meeting customer expectations.** This first level of customer satisfaction occurs when your customer receives exactly what he expected to receive when he bought your product or service.

2. **Exceeding customer expectations.** You move customers to the second level of satisfaction when you do something that is even more than the customer expected.

3. **Delighting your customers.** When you delight your customers, you do or say something that is completely unexpected and that makes the customer feel happy. Whereas meeting customer expectations will ensure that you stay in business, and exceeding customer expectations is essential to future growth and profitability, when you start *delighting* your customer you put yourself on the side of the angels. When you deliver customer satisfaction at this third level, that's when customers start thinking that "This is a great business" and become more inclined to patronize you again in the future.

4. **Amazing your customers.** The fourth level of customer satisfaction is where you do or say something that is so positive and unusual that your customer is amazed. When your customers are so delighted and amazed with the way you treated them, they start telling other people about you and either send or bring you new customers so that they can have the same experience that the customer has enjoyed. Delighting *and* amazing your customers leads to perhaps the highest level of customer satisfaction, which is "customer advocacy."

Measure *Their* Expectations, Not Just Yours

Be careful how you measure success so that you are really meeting *your customers'* expectations, not yours. Following is an experience coauthor Mark had, which illustrates this point.

Mark: I drove through Jack in the Box on a busy day and got a big surprise. The staffer took our order, took our money, and then asked me to drive away.

"Excuse me?" I asked, a bit surprised.

"Sorry, we have to move you through quickly. We need you to get out of the way," she continued as if I was somehow out of the loop on fast food protocol.

I was speechless. "Please pull forward and park over to the right," she ordered. Then she was gone.

I sat for a moment. There wasn't room to park on the right. It was a narrow drive-through lane with a curb on one side and then the traffic zooming past on the street. I squeezed the car forward and up onto the curb. Putting on my emergency flashers, I walked back to the window before the next car could pull up.

"We will be right with you," she admonished me as I approached. I smiled and explained that I didn't realize that drive-through meant I was to drop money and leave. I said I would stand there until the manager came to me with our "fast food."

The franchise owner sighed and stepped forward. He explained that his understanding of the Jack in the Box system was that it was meant to measure who quickly customers are processed through. Well, it was efficient but hardly effective.

"That's how all the stores do it—we compete with each other," he claimed, exasperated. He was gaming the measurement system on how fast they could move the customer, not the food.

That clearly is *not* how Jack in the Box intended this measurement to be used. But the fact that it can get confused out in the field means that it's a good habit for you to "mystery shop" your own stores on busy days to see what really happens. You have to be careful what you wish for: What kinds of behaviors are your measurement systems actually rewarding? Is it improving the customer experience? People tend to go after the incentives using the letter, not the spirit, of the law you put in place.

The irony is that one Dictionary.com definition of the word *customer* unintentionally captures that fast-food manager's bad attitude:

cus·tom·er   A person one has to deal with. . . .

Yes, you do have to *deal* with customers. It's ironic how often we run across customer service organizations that resent customers and think providing service is an imposition. That is why great companies know that the key to great customer experiences is to hire people who love customers and love service. It's essential to find service people who get an energy lift from making customers happy—people who are delighted to look for and discover the deep subconscious needs they can satisfy for your customers. The satisfaction of these needs are the building blocks of all relationships.

The Three A's

1. **Acceptance.** Each person has a deep down need to be accepted *unconditionally* by other people. One of the greatest fears that people have is the fear of rejection, of being criticized or not respected by others. One of the greatest joys is to be completely accepted by another person or by everyone you meet.

The way that you and your customer service team should express acceptance is simple. Smile! (This may seem obvious, but it must not be since you don't see enough of this behavior!) When you smile at people, you improve their self-image and raise their self-esteem. You make them feel more valuable, respected, and worthwhile. When you smile at another person, that person glows inside and feels happy to be in your presence. If you are on the phone, put a mirror there and smile into it so your customer can hear the smile in your voice.

Whenever you have a "moment of truth" or a contact with new or existing customers, you should act as if you are glad to see them. You should brighten up and smile and be welcoming, as if you were running into a long-lost friend after many years. You should make your customers feel glad that they met you and spoke to you.

Remember the halo effect. The first customer contact that a person has sets a tone that can either shine a light or cast a shadow over the rest of the customer relationship. In business, be sure that whoever answers the phone or speaks to the customer is a positive, courteous, friendly, cheerful, and pleasant person to talk to.

2. **Appreciation.** Every human being has a deep need to be recognized, to feel significant. Whenever you express appreciation to another person, that person feels more valuable and important. Appreciation has an emotional impact on people; their self-image improves and their self-esteem increases. Appreciation makes them feel better about themselves, and to like you by extension.

How do you express appreciation? It's simple. Say "thank you." Take every opportunity to thank your customers for calling you or buying from you. Thank them for coming in and thank them when they leave. Phone them and leave thank-you messages on their voicemail or answering machines. Send thank-you notes and cards after a purchase or transaction.

Continually think of additional ways, large and small, to say *thank you* to your customers for doing business with you. Because this kind of gesture is often unexpected, it will both delight and amaze your customers and cause them to come back to you over and over again, and bring their friends, too.

3. **Attention.** You demonstrate attention when you *listen intently* to your customers as they express their feelings or opinions to you. Listening has been called "white magic" because of the incredible power and influence it has over the person being listened to. When you listen intently to people when they

are expressing their thoughts or feelings, their self-esteem goes up. They feel more valuable and important. They feel happy inside.

When you listen intently, the other person will consider *you* to be a more valuable and more worthwhile person as well. Paying close attention to your customers, listening to them without interrupting or attempting to interrupt, has a completely positive effect on your customers and their feelings about you and your offerings. Because of the halo effect, they unconsciously assume that your company is better managed, and that your customer service is superior, and that your products and services are superior to those of your competitors and worth more money.

Love Your Customers

One of the most powerful and important competitive advantages you can develop is the quality of the relationships with your customers. The most successful and profitable businesses, of all kinds, at all levels of business activity, are those companies that care about and take care of their customers better than anyone else.

What would you do differently in your business if you truly loved your customers? Imagine that your customers were personally responsible for paying your paycheck, assuring your lifestyle with your family, paying for your car, vacations, restaurant meals, clothes, and all the good things you enjoy in life. Imagine also that your customers provided you with all of these things completely spontaneously, without asking anything in return, other than that your products and services do what they say they will do, and continue to do it, after they buy them.

If you felt this powerful emotional bond with customers, how would you encourage your staff to treat them?

How would loving your customers change your product or service offerings, or your delivery, if your staff truly loved your customers?

By taking care of your customers exactly the way that you would like to be taken care of *if you were a customer,* you can continually trigger those wonderful words: "This is a great business!"

This Is Your Legacy

When you decide to build a great team of people to create an extraordinary customer experience, you are ready to develop all of the potential possibilities for your business. As they say in the army, "You can be all you can be." You can fulfill your hopes, achieve your goals, and make a significant contribution to yourself, your family, your company, and your society.

"I'd rather be ashes than dust," said author Jack London. *Run, don't walk,* into your future. There is no better time than right now, today, to put all your energy into building your dreams and creating a better, bigger, more profitable business.

This is the greatest opportunity of your lifetime. Don't let it slip past.

Now, go and build a great business!

CHAPTER 7 CHECKLIST FOR CREATING A GREAT CUSTOMER EXPERIENCE

1. What are the **promises you make** when you ask a customer to trust you and to buy your products and services?

   a. _____

   b. _____

   c. _____

2. What are the **promises you keep** after a customer has bought from you?

   a. _____

   b. _____

   c. _____

3. List three things that you do today to create a **great customer experience:**

   a. _____

   b. _____

   c. _____

4. List three things that you and **your customers love** about your competitor's customer experience:

   a. _____

   b. _____

   c. _____

5. List the three most positive things that **customers say** about you, your people, and your products and services:

    a. _____

    b. _____

    c. _____

6. List your three most common **customer complaints** and what you can do to resolve them:

    a. _____

    b. _____

    c. _____

7. What are the **three A's** of customer relationships, and how can you incorporate them into every customer experience?

    a. _____

    b. _____

    c. _____

    What **one action** are you going to take immediately to create a great customer experience based on your answers to the previous seven questions?

    _____

    _____

    _____

Now, Build a Great Life!

"The things that matter most must never be at the mercy of the things that matter least."

—GOETHE

While building a great business and maximizing profits are important goals, your main goal should be to live a *great* life. You have to fix your own life before you can fix your business or become a productive business leader.

Regardless of short-term economic fluctuations, we are living in the very best time in all of human history. There are more opportunities and possibilities for more people to achieve more of their goals in the years ahead than have every existed before.

Your goal should be to be one of those people.

The starting point of living a great life is for you to decide exactly what a great life would be like for you if you could create it. As they say, "You've got to have a dream if you want to make a dream come true." We call this practice *future orientation.*

Future Orientation

Top people think about the future most of the time. To create a great life, you must think and act the way great men and women have thought and acted throughout the ages. You must think and imagine the way they did (and still do), and soon you'll get the same results.

As Wayne Dyer said, "You will see it when you believe it, not the other way around."

Practice Idealization

Imagine that you could be, have, or do anything you wanted in the years ahead. What would it be? Imagine that you have a magic wand and that you can wave it and create any kind of future you desire. How would it be different from today?

You begin the process of *idealization* by imagining that you have no limitations. Imagine that you have all the time and money, all the knowledge and skill, all the education and experience, and all the friends and contacts that you would ever need. If you had no limitations, what kind of a "five-year fantasy" would you create for yourself?

Begin with your business, career, and income. If you were working in the perfect business five years from today, what would it look like? How would it be different from today?

If you were earning your ideal income, doing the kind of work that you most enjoy, with the kind of people that you really like, at the position to which you aspire, what would it look like? How would it be different from today? And what could you do, starting today, to begin creating your ideal future vision of your work and career?

The Ultimate Personal Life

Think about your family and your personal life. If you could wave a magic wand and create a perfect family situation five years from today, how would it be different? What kind of home would you live in, and where would it be located? What kind of lifestyle would you have, day in and day out? What kind of things would you like to do for and with your family? What kind of vacations and trips would you take?

To create your perfect lifestyle, what steps would you have to take to get from where you are today to where you want to be some time in the future? Most of all, what step could you take immediately to begin making your future vision a reality?

Think about your health. If your health was perfect in every way, how would it be different from today? How much would you weigh, how much would you exercise, and what level of fitness would you have? What kind of energy would you have and what kind of activities would you engage in if you were physically fit and healthy in every respect?

What would be the first step that you could take immediately to begin creating a superbly healthy lifestyle?

Your Best Financial Condition

Finally, consider your financial situation. You can't hit a target that you can't see. The greater clarity you have regarding where you want to end up in your financial life, the more likely it is that you will achieve that goal.

To achieve financial independence, you begin by determining your "exact number." This is the amount that you will want to have saved, invested, and working for you when you retire. As Barbara De Angelis once asked, "How much will you need to be satisfied, and what will you do then?"

You calculate your number by determining how much money you would have to have to support your current lifestyle if you had no income at all. Add up your rent, payments, groceries, travel expenses, medical expenses, and so on to determine your monthly "nut."

How Much Would You Need?

You then ask yourself how long you could survive on your current savings and investments if your income was cut off today. This tells you what your current "burn rate" is and how long you could survive.

Once you have determined your minimum monthly financial requirement, multiply that number by 12 to determine how much you would need if your income was cut off for a year. This may seem simplistic—and it is—but it's amazing how few people at any level of income or wealth actually take the time to create a budget that sets aside funds for their particular lifestyle. We have seen multimillionaires fail at this as often as those who are just building their nest egg. Once you get clear about how much money you really think you need, you'll find it reduces stress and makes you more effective.

Finally, multiply the annual amount times 20 to determine your "number," which is the amount that you will need to have saved, invested, and working for you at the time you retire. To simplify this equation, you can multiply your monthly requirement by 240 to get your target for financial accumulation and financial independence.

Planning for the Rest of Your Life

The average lifespan is about eighty years, and it is increasing each year. Since you are going to be enjoying excellent health, you should plan to live for another twenty years after you retire. Investment advisers suggest that you should be able to draw down your accumulated savings at the rate of 4 percent or 5 percent per year indefinitely and never run out of money. This is your goal.

Once you have determined your long-term financial goal, you come back to the present and determine exactly what you are worth today. Imagine that you are going to sell everything you have and move to a foreign country. How much would you be left with?

You then draw a graph with your current net worth at the lower left hand corner and your desired net worth at the upper right hand corner. You divide this graph vertically into five-year blocks, and then one-year blocks, so that you are clear about how much you will have to earn, save, invest, and accumulate each year to achieve your goal.

One of the most effective ways to build your retirement fund is to save—to actually set aside 10 percent of your income every month. This approach will accumulate assets surprisingly fast. No matter what level of your income, or how great or small your savings, it is important to set aside savings every month. It may feel impossible when things are tight, but the sooner you try to make savings a regular practice, the better off you will be and the sooner you will reach your dreams.

Take That Leap of Faith

Then take action. The first step is always the hardest; it's a leap of faith into the unknown because there are never any guarantees that anything will work out exactly as you planned. Until you take the first step nothing happens.

The good news is that, when you take that initial action, you immediately get feedback that enables you to self-correct. You start to get input, ideas, and insights that will help you move more intelligently toward your goals. As you begin to make forward progress, you start to feel more energy and enthusiasm. Your brain releases endorphins, nature's "happy drug," and you feel happy at the sensation of forward progress.

When you take the first step, you will see far enough to take the next step. If you remain clear about your goal, but flexible about the process of achieving it, you will always see at least one step ahead. You will always know what to do next.

Goal-Setting Formula

A second orientation that you need to live a great life is *goal orientation*. This means that you have clear specific written goals for what you want to accomplish in the months and years ahead.

Take a clean sheet of paper and make a list of ten goals that you would like to accomplish in the next year or so. Use the three-P formula: present tense, positive, and personal.

1. **Present tense.** Always write your goals in the present tense, as though a year has passed and you have already accomplished the goal. Instead of saying "I will earn $XXX," you say, "I earn $XXX dollars over the next twelve months."

2. **Positive tone.** Write your goals using a positive tone rather than a negative one. Instead of saying "I will quit smoking," say, "I am a nonsmoker" (positive and present tense).

3. **Personal action.** Make it personal. There are two ways to do this. For many people, it's most effective to begin each goal statement with the word "I" followed by an action verb—"*I* have a thirty-four-inch waist." Other people may prefer to address themselves as "You" with each goal statement. Try saying, "*You* are enjoying your brand-new office" or "*You* have achieved your goal."

The shorter and more precise your goal statements— starting with the word "I," followed by an action verb, in the present tense with a positive tone—the more rapidly they are accepted by your subconscious mind. Once your goals are programmed into your consciousness (which is the reason for writing them down), your subconscious and superconscious minds go to work to bring them into your life twenty-four hours a day.

Once you have made a list of ten present, positive, personal-tense goals, go over your list and imagine that you could accomplish the goals on this list sooner or later—as long as you wanted them badly enough. But imagine also that you could accomplish any one goal on this list within twenty-four hours.

What One Goal Matters Most Now?

Here's the question: What one goal, if you could accomplish it in twenty-four hours, would have the greatest positive impact on your life? We are not asking this question to push you to actually achieve that goal in a day, but rather to consider what would make the most satisfying difference in your life and work.

Whatever that goal, put a circle around it, and move it to the top of a clean sheet of paper. There is a simple seven-step process for achieving goals like this one that you can use for the rest of your life.

Seven-Step Process for Achieving Goals

Step 1: Make it measurable. Decide exactly what you want. Be specific and make it measureable. Your goal should be so clear that a ten-year-old child could tell you how close you are to achieving it.

Step 2: Write it down. Give it concrete form. People with written goals accomplish ten times as much as people who only have wishes and hopes.

Step 3: Set a deadline. You need a target to aim at if you want to achieve your goal. If your goal is big enough, set subdeadlines as well.

Step 4: Make a list of tasks. List everything that you can think of that you could possibly do to achieve your goal. As you think of new tasks and activities, write them down until your list is complete.

Step 5: Prioritize. Organize the list by both sequence and priority. Arrange your list in the right sequence by determining what you will have to do first, before you move on to do something else. Organize your list by priority by determining what is more important and what is less important.

A list that is organized by sequence and priority is a plan. *Voila!* Now you have a goal and a plan, in writing. You are now ready to supercharge your future.

Step 6: Take action on your plan immediately. Do something. Do anything. Step out in faith. Think of any cliché that motivates you. Put the ball into play, but don't swing for the fences the first time at bat. Make it a small step that is fairly easy to achieve. Go get some information or interview someone who does what you are hoping to do. Feel the energy and get some insights from someone you admire. The very act of taking action on your goal begins a mental and an emotional process that can transform your life.

Step 7: Make daily progress. Do something every day that moves you forward. Seven days a week, 365 days a year, do something, anything that moves you a little bit in the right direction. Small moves matter. This sense of forward momentum will energize and empower you and eventually make you unstoppable and irresistible.

Action Creates Attraction

The final key to building a great life is *action orientation*. The ultimate law of attraction says that when you apply the law of action first, you put into motion everything that demonstrates to other people (and further convinces yourself) that you are excited about your future. Nothing is more infectious than your excitement about doing what matters to you.

All successful people are intensely action oriented. They are in constant motion. They try, try again, and then try something else. They believe in "doing it, fixing it, trying it."

The Law of Probabilities

Success in life is more a result of the law of probabilities than of the law of attraction or plain luck. The law of probability says that there is a probability that anything can happen, including your achieving your most important goals. This law also says that "the more things that you try, the more likely it is that you will triumph."

The more actions you take in the direction of your goals, the greater the probability that you will achieve that goal. The more things that you learn and try, the faster you move, the more ground you cover, and the more likely you are to achieve your most important goal on schedule.

Spiral of Energy

The faster you move, the more energy you have. The faster you move, the more ground you cover and the more experience you get. The faster you move, the more likely you are to succeed. The more you succeed, the more motivated you will be to take more actions, try more things, and cover more ground. When you put your life onto an upward spiral of energy, enthusiasm, motivation, and ultimate success, nothing will be able to stop you.

Realize that there are no limits in life except the limits that you impose on yourself with your own thinking. Believe in yourself. Believe in your unlimited possibilities. Believe that the only thing standing between you and what you want to accomplish are your own doubts and fears.

The truth is that you can do, be, and have anything that you put your mind to. Decide what you want, write it down, make a plan, and take action today.

Now, build a great life!

Index

Now... Build a Great Business! — FREE Resources

Brian Tracy and Mark Thompson have created these resources to help you get a step ahead in your business and your life.

Strategic Planning Business Blueprint PDF

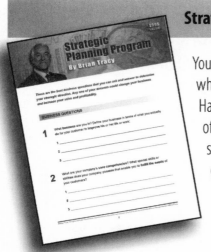

You don't have to be a certified business guru to know what's working within your business and what's not. Having a clear and detailed strategic plan is the basis of your business success. This detailed and practical strategic planning guide will help you identify your goals and create a business blueprint for achieving them — faster than ever before!

Free E-Book with Video Insights

DOUBLE YOUR VALUE!
Seven Ways to Be More Valuable to Your Company, Your Customers, and Everyone Who Matters

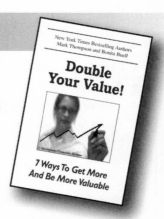

Learn how you can become worth more to the people who matter most to your future success. In this e-book, you'll receive secret tips and links to video insights from the world's top executive recruiters and extraordinary leaders like Virgin's Richard Branson, Pepsico's Indra Nooyi, Ford's Alan Mulally, Zappos' Tony Hsieh and leadership guru Jim Collins.

The Art of Closing the Sale

aving the ability to close a sale is the most
nportant skill anyone in business can possess.
'hether you're selling your own products or
rvices, or someone in your company is selling
em for you, sales is an integral part of any
usiness's success. Brian Tracy's audio program
ownload, The Art of Closing the Sale, will teach you
e most effective closing techniques so you can boost your
rofits and increase sales in your business.

12 Step Goal Setting Process plus Exercise

In planning for success you always start with yourself and
your personal goals. Your work and your business life are
what you do so you can enjoy the most important parts
of your life – your family and your relationships.

This 12 Step Goal Setting Process and Goal Setting
Exercise will help you determine what is really
important to you so that you can make better
decisions in your business and personal life.

Now...
GO Build a Great Business!

Visit www.briantracy.com/greatbusiness

for your **FREE** resources.

BUILD A GREAT BUSINESS!

BRIAN TRACY'S TOTAL BUSINESS MAKEOVER

(2½ Day Live Seminar/Workshop)

If you liked this book, *Now, Build a Great Business!,* you're going to love this seminar.

In this two and a half day **Total Business Makeover,** Brian Tracy and his team of experts not only expand on the revolutionary ideas in this book but cover two additional powerful principles of business.

In this live training you cover each area of *Now, Build a Great Business!* in further detail while you work on your own personal Action Guide.

You'll work on your business and talk with peers and experts about your challenges, successes, goals, and ideas. You'll leave this seminar with a written plan for success in your business.

Plus you get additional information on how to become a great business person and how to generate great numbers.

Working on a combination of what Brian Tracy calls "the ten essential areas of business success" will enable you to make your business a success and achieve all your financial goals.

This seminar is not only perfect for people who are already in business and who want to grow faster, it is also ideal for anyone thinking about starting a business for the first time.

For more information, go to
www.briantracy.com/tbm2 or call 858-436-7300.

Learn the practical, proven skills and techniques
you need to survive, thrive and grow
in any business and in any market. . . .